EVEN
WITH MY
ISSUES

DR. WANDA A. TURNER

W

WHITAKER
HOUSE

Unless otherwise indicated, all Scripture quotations are taken from the King James Version (KJV) of the Bible.

Scripture quotations marked (NKJV) are taken from the *New King James Version*, © 1979, 1980, 1982 by Thomas Nelson, Inc. Used by permission. All rights reserved.

Editorial note: Even at the cost of violating grammatical rules, we have chosen not to capitalize the name satan and related names.

EVEN WITH MY ISSUES

For speaking engagements, contact Dr. Wanda A. Turner at:
Covenant Worship Center
425 South La Brea Ave.
Inglewood, CA 90301
e-mail: DRLADYT@aol.com
web site: drwandaturner.com

ISBN: 0-88368-673-2
Printed in the United States of America
© 2001 by Dr. Wanda A. Turner

Whitaker House
30 Hunt Valley Circle
New Kensington, PA 15068
web site: whitakerhouse.com

Library of Congress Cataloging-in-Publication Data

Turner, Wanda A., 1948–
  Even with my issues / by Wanda A. Turner.
    p. cm.
  ISBN 0-88368-673-2 (pbk. : alk. paper)
  1. Christian life. 2. Suffering—Religious aspects—Christianity. 3. Sins. I. Title.
  BV4909 .T87 2001
  248.4—dc21   2001004481

2 3 4 5 6 7 8 9 10 11 12 / 09 08 07 06 05 04 03 02

Dedication

*I*t is my desire that this book will speak to every man, woman, boy, and girl who believes the untruth that the issues in their lives will abort, interrupt, and or frustrate their destined success in life!

There is a Power, a Resource, and a marvelous Support provided for you, and you, and you that will loose you from pain, shame, defeat, and death!

I dedicate this book to the memory of Cokie, Eric, Eugene, Hosea, Tasha, Michael, and Harold.

Table of Contents

Acknowledgments

T his was probably one of the toughest books for me to write. Somehow, from start to finish, I knew it would be special—a unique as well as a powerful tool in the hands of hurting people who are ready to do something positive and powerful about the pain in their lives called issues!

I appreciate the encouragement of Rosalyn Harris, the critical and timely assistance of Michelle Jones, the support of my husband, ACT II, and my inspiration...the Lord Jesus Christ!

Special thanks to the Whitaker House family, especially Jim Rill, Sharon Hemingway, and Thom Gardner, who believed in this project from its inception and helped to bring it to fruition.

—WANDA A. TURNER

Introduction

*O*ne night as I lay asleep after having just returned
from a long ministry trip, a gentle yet persistent
voice awakened me. "Wanda...Wanda." I was not
immediately sure who was speaking to me. I mumbled,
"No, please don't...I'm not ready to get up yet. The flight
from Los Angeles was so long last night." But the voice
persisted until finally I realized that it was the voice of
the Spirit calling to me.

"Yes, Lord," I replied.

"Wanda, I want to speak with you. Slip out of bed quietly and come into the bathroom."

Moving carefully so as not to wake my husband, I
rolled out of bed and grabbed my newly purchased
journal, my oft-used, worn Bible, and a pen from the
nightstand. I felt my way through the darkness into the

bathroom, quietly shut the door behind me, and turned on the light. As I sat on the floor, the Spirit of God led me to open my Bible to the fifth chapter of Mark. At first it was as if my Bible was an aged photo album filled with the sepia tones of old-fashioned, tintype pictures. But as I read, the Lord allowed me to see those scenes in light of my own life, and they were transformed into the vivid colors of a modern Kodak print.

I began scribbling notes in my journal—notes that would change my life forever—words that would reach beyond my life to touch the lives of others. As I read, listening to the Spirit of God, my eyes lit upon these words: *"And a certain woman, which had an issue...she... touched...[Jesus]...and...she was healed"* (Mark 5:25, 27, 29). As I read those words, I could feel the anointing of the Lord flowing over me like warm oil. Then the voice of the Spirit began to speak to my spirit.

"Wanda, you must help My people to identify the issues that have kept them from Me. Identify them, but don't try to heal them yourself. You must bring the people to Me. They must be allowed to come to Me, to touch Me, issues and all. You have no power to heal My children. Only as they reach out to Me in faith can they be made whole. Let them touch Me."

I realized that the Lord had spoken powerfully to me. I would have to rethink my entire belief system about the issues, failures, faults, sins, and troubles that reside in the lives of people in the kingdom of God. I discovered, as I read the words in Mark 5, that a shifting is necessary in the body of Christ. We need to cease dealing with surface

matters and begin to deal with the wounds and issues deep in the hearts of those in the church.

The Spirit was telling me of a new era in the church—an era in which people would reach out to touch the hem of Christ's garment and be healed. And the healing they receive will put the glory of God on display for all the world to see—resulting in praise and worship in the presence of God. For they will be healed not by the ministry or intervention of man, but by the presence of Christ!

The church has kept more people away from Christ and healing than it has brought to Him. We have offered teaching and doctrine, but we have not brought the needy to Christ so that they might touch Him and be healed. Only Jesus can make them whole—but it is up to them to reach out to Him. No issue has ever been settled by touching man.

We must recognize that we all have issues. I have issues; you have issues. Once we realize that, we are ready for the next question: Are we ready to leave the guilt and shame and separation behind and be healed? God wants to do a new thing in our old lives. He wants us to reach out to Him. Will we? Jesus is waiting in the midst of that crowd. We must push, press, run, walk or crawl—we must do whatever we have to do to get to Jesus. He desires to touch us and heal us *even with our issues.*

Chapter One

---·∞·---

Even with
My Issues

Chapter One

Even with My Issues

And a certain woman, which had an issue of blood twelve years, and had suffered many things of many physicians, and had spent all that she had, and was nothing bettered, but rather grew worse, when she had heard of Jesus, came in the press behind, and touched his garment. For she said, If I may touch but his clothes, I shall be whole. And straightway the fountain of her blood was dried up; and she felt in her body that she was healed of that plague. And Jesus, immediately knowing in himself that virtue had gone out of him, turned him about in the press, and said, Who touched my clothes? And his disciples said unto him, Thou seest the multitude thronging thee, and sayest thou, Who touched me? And he looked round about to see her that had done this thing. But the woman fearing and trembling, knowing what was done in her, came and fell down before him, and told him all the truth. And he

said unto her, Daughter, thy faith hath made thee whole; go in peace, and be whole of thy plague.
—Mark 5:25–34

She was separated and alone, day after day, month after month, and year after year. She felt no physical contact, no warm touch from another human being. Her very presence caused some who knew of her condition to recoil so as to avoid contamination. For twelve years, life hemorrhaged from her body, leaving her pale and weak and rendering her unclean in the eyes of those in her family and community. She was alone and cut off, hearing only the whispering voice of her own self-condemnation.

Then, after many years, the monotony of her seclusion was interrupted by the swell of discussion concerning One through whom miracles and healing flowed. Her village of Capernaum was alive with reports concerning Jesus, a Rabbi transplanted from Nazareth who was said to have healed the sick and calmed storm-tossed seas. Could this be her season of healing? If He had healed others with a word, could He not speak that word to her as well? If He could calm a raging sea, why not her unsettled heart?

This was a time of desperate hope for her. She had invested the little money she had in one false hope after another to rid herself of her plague. There was not a counselor or a quack who did not know her and seek to sell her a remedy. After trying everything they had to offer, she only got worse. Now all of her money and reasonable hopes were gone, yet the stories concerning this

One who brought deliverance stirred a new hope in her heart. With the walls of her confinement closing in about her, she realized that she could no longer live with this condition, with this issue. She had to act.

Outside her door was heard the sound of a gathering throng seeking release from their own concerns. There were the sick and the depressed, the poor and the disfigured, all streaming toward Jesus. As the procession ebbed past her door, she asked herself, "Why should I not join them?" Her secret could be well disguised. She would be just one more face in a sea of faces. Besides, those in the crowd were so focused on obtaining their own blessing that no one would notice her. So with her heart filled with equal amounts of hope and fear, she stepped across the threshold of her seclusion and into the sea of seekers. Now this one, who for so many years had remained anonymous, was caught in the undertow of human desperation and swept toward the Source of all healing and life.

Around her a forest of arms and hands stretched and strained to receive something from Jesus. There were the hands of fishermen, rough and callous from years of work and wear. There were the gnarled hands of old women stricken with arthritis and age. There were hands of hungry children and hurting humanity reaching out from every direction and angle. The people swarmed Jesus like bees to honey. Then, in a moment of desperation, her eyes focused on the tassel tied to the corner of His garment—the holiest portion of His clothing. The blue and white tassel hung from the corner of His outer vestment, between His shoulder blades

and over His heart. This was the representation of all that was holy—the emblem of God's law and covenant faithfulness to His people. Her heart pounded as rationale gave way to impulse. Before she could think, in a moment of blind and desperate trust, she thrust her hand through the sea of hands and laid hold of the fringe of His garment.

Suddenly, something surged though her body. In an instant a rush of power coursed through her to the very root of her defilement, and immediately the flow of her life's blood was stopped. She reached out deliberately to Jesus in her *defilement*. She reached out to Him in utter *destitution*. She reached out to Him in her *desperation*. And the instant she laid hold of His garment, Jesus removed the very source of all three.

Jesus was aware of the flow of power out of Him to someone in the crowd. With so many crowding and grabbing at Him, how could He know who had received the virtue that issued from His person? He turned suddenly and asked, "Who touched Me?" Now her face, which only a moment earlier had been pale and white, was blushed with the vigor of newly returned life. She stood there trembling in amazement at what the Lord had done in her. She realized that she could no longer hide what had happened to her, so she threw herself at the feet of Jesus. For a few moments she recounted her life to Him, telling all that had happened to her, from plague to purity. When she had confessed it all, Jesus pronounced her whole, saying, "Shalom! You have been made whole. Go and live a whole life!" Her issue was settled in Jesus.

We All Have Issues

All of us have secret issues that hinder us, secret struggles that keep us barren and hidden. These issues drain the abundant life from us. Just as we are about to get a big promotion at work, the issue of fear comes up and we back away. Or maybe we are at the beginning of a God-ordained relationship when an issue of past shame or guilt derails us. Regardless of the specific issue, all of us experience limitations in our walk in the kingdom of God. And as with this woman's issue, there can be only one answer, only one way to settle our issue: We must reach out to Jesus Christ.

What exactly is an issue? An issue is a condition, an attitude, or a circumstance that robs us of the abundant life that Jesus has secured for us. These issues can include, but are not limited to, such things as pride, poverty, fear, rebellion, and physical limitations. Issues are those private, secret things of our past and present that show up to hinder, block, trouble, hold hostage, abort, and even destroy our dreams, hopes, and desires. They are the challenges, problems, and crises that attach themselves to us (sometimes generationally) to block our success, victory, and effectiveness in the kingdom of God. Issues show up without invitation. They are like a run in a new pair of nylons or a flat tire on a new car—frustrating and costly.

The word *issue* has become a hip term in current "psychobabble." Where before we may have referred to someone as having a "besetting sin or weight," now we declare that "So-and-so has some major unresolved

issues." And while we point accusing fingers at everyone else, we overlook the fact that we are lugging around the heavy baggage of our own issues.

How do we discover our own issues? How can we describe them? What do they look like? Here are several characteristics of those things we are describing as *issues.*

Issues are private, secret "stuff." Issues are those uniquely personal things that we try to hide, eliminate, or at least push off to the side and out of the way. But on our own, we do not have the strength, courage, or intellect to do so. Out of shame and fear, we hide these problems from everyone and pray that no one will discover the secret wounds and imperfections that make us vulnerable.

Issues cause separation. As with the woman in Mark's gospel, issues keep us separated from God and people. We tend to keep them to ourselves and may even hide them under a facade of humor or aloofness. We do not go out into the "marketplace" to form new relationships or become involved in ministry. And each time we begin to speak to God in prayer, we do so through a veil of religious form and ritual. Our issues do not allow us to become intimate and vulnerable with God or those who live around us.

Issues always flow from a source. Vine's Complete Expository Dictionary states that the noun *issue* is from the Greek word *rhusis,* meaning "a flowing." Issues such as fear, anger, or bitterness flow from a source somewhere deep in our past experience and belief system.

So until we deal with the source of these issues, they will continue to flow throughout our lives. It is up to us whether we go through the same frustrating dilemmas over and over, or whether we gain victory over them in Christ Jesus and move on to face new and exciting challenges.

Issues result in character qualities that limit our lives. Not everything that happens in our lives is an issue, nor do we have to make an issue out of everything. Circumstances don't become issues until they appear repeatedly in our lives. For example, if your car gets a flat tire and you have to call AAA, that's a circumstance. But if you're calling AAA every other day to give you a tow because you haven't given your vehicle regular maintenance, that's an issue of character.

Issues elicit strong emotions. The strongest emotion that people with issues experience is fear—usually the fear of rejection if their issue is exposed. This fear can be accompanied by shame, guilt, anger, and frustration, which in turn can lead to hopelessness and despair. On the other hand, our issues may trigger emotional reactions in others as well, such as disapproval, prejudice, hate, arrogance, judgment, condemnation, and rejection. In reality, our issues trigger the issues of other people, making it virtually impossible to have normal and open relationships with others.

Issues are unwelcome. These challenging problems, predicaments, and crises are unsolicited and unwelcome. They seem to appear out of nowhere, but in reality the groundwork that allows them to take hold of us may

have been laid in the past. Some issues are inherited tendencies from generational curses, while others may be the result of bad choices we made years ago. Some issues may even be the work of the enemy to slow down our effective ministry.

Issues affect our everyday lives and personalities. As we carry our issues with us year after year, we begin to adapt our lives to them. The woman with the issue of blood had adapted and limited her entire existence around the secret issue that plagued her. The saying goes that a chain is only as strong as its weakest link. In a similar way, our lives will be only as effective as the issues that we carry. Too often we walk through life in a spiritual paranoia, allowing our issues to direct our paths.

Issues result in bondage. Some issues become like one of those Chinese finger cuffs we played with as kids. You put your two index fingers in opposite ends of this woven tubular mesh and then try to pull them apart. The harder you try, the tighter the cuff becomes. Similarly, we want to be free of our issues, but we attempt to manage them in our own strength rather than reach out to the grace of God in Christ Jesus. And the more we wrestle with these issues in our own strength, the tighter and more restrictive they become. We cannot get free using our own capabilities!

Issues often become excuses. Many wonderful and talented people headed for greatness in the kingdom instead find themselves detoured by issues onto side roads marked, "Woulda," "Coulda," and "Shoulda." Too many are heard saying, "I could have been great, but,

well, you know my issue!" Instead of dealing with those issues that limit them, they continue traveling the detour, heading further away from their dreams and hopes.

Issues tend to attract more issues. Although issues can be general or specific, brand name or generic, they have a habit of attaching themselves to certain people—those men, women, boys, and girls who are distinct, uniquely gifted, and destined for greatness. The higher the degree of talent and skill, promise and potential that a person has, the more likely he or she is to have multiple issues. Issues seem to cluster together and seek out the best and brightest people to plague.

Issues are part of a deliberate enemy strategy. Frequently, issues are demonic, diabolical assignments from the pit of hell. They bind and gag our present and future, holding us mute and immobile with the ropes of past failures. They ride into our consciousness on guilt and shame, whispering soft and sickening reminders of our defilement and unworthiness. They keep us cowering in the dark and away from the grace of God.

This list of characteristics could go on, but I think you get the basic idea. The bottom line is, our issues hold us captive in the dark, separate and ineffective, until they are brought out into the light and dealt with in the power of the cross.

It is not enough just to know that we all have issues; that knowledge alone is enough to depress us and become another issue itself. No, we must understand that we can be free of the issues that plague us. Furthermore, we must realize that even while we struggle to be free of

our issues, God still loves us and draws us into His kingdom.

Yes, we all have issues, but the kingdom of God goes on. *Even with our issues* we are involved in the Father's business and the ministry of the kingdom. Even with our limitations and gross imperfections, we are somehow still useful to God. But how can a holy God use imperfect people like us, riddled with issues? It's simple. God restores us in *His* strength, to work *His* purposes, in *His* power.

It was not until the woman with the issue of blood was drained of her own strength and resources that she reached out to Jesus in a hopeful desperation. You see, His power could not flow into her and heal her issue until she was empty. So it was out of her own defilement, destitution, and desperation that she reached out to Jesus. In the same way, the power of Christ is perfected in us as we reach out to Him in our weakness. We do not minister in our strength, but out of His. We do not minister in our wisdom; we minister the One who is wisdom. We minister His life out of our own death. The apostle Paul declared,

> And he said unto me, My grace is sufficient for thee: for my strength is made perfect in weakness. Most gladly therefore will I rather glory in my infirmities, that the power of Christ may rest upon me.
> (2 Corinthians 12:9)

Dealing with Our Issues

How do we find healing for the issues in our lives? How can they be "dried up" as the woman's issue was?

The gospel narrative provides us with a hammer and chisel to break the bonds of our limitations. Mark 5 gives us three imperatives to follow if we are to find healing and wholeness for our issues. I have reduced these to three words: *exhausted, enlightened,* and *entrusting.*

Exhausted

We must come to the point where our resources are exhausted; we have to realize that we cannot heal ourselves, that only Jesus can heal us. The woman with the issue of blood spent all that she had. There was no place left to go, no solution to be found by human means and human wisdom. Today we try to counsel one another out of our issues and make ourselves feel better about our problems. At best such counseling deals with the symptoms, but rarely with the roots of our issues. It is not enough for us to deal with the symptoms or the results of our strongholds; we must find out where they are founded and established.

For example, if a man walked into a hospital with an arrow stuck in his chest, it would not be enough to give him an aspirin for the pain and then send him to a counselor to learn how to manage life with an arrow stuck in his chest. No, the only way to bring real and lasting healing is to turn him over to a surgeon and have the doctor remove the arrow. In the same way, we must turn ourselves over to Jesus. He alone knows the sources and roots of our issues, and He alone can remove them. They could be rooted in some past abuse or trauma. They could be rooted in a generational curse or habit. Whatever its source, an issue will not cease to flow until we deal with it at the source.

Enlightened

Issues must be brought out into the light, enlightened by the Son of God, in order to be healed. Issues will never miraculously vanish on their own; they will not fade away by themselves. Issues will always reappear until they are submitted to the light of Christ to be dealt with. Our issues must be touched by a Power greater than ourselves. They must be challenged, sometimes ruthlessly, to come out of hiding so that they can be dealt with once and for all. Exposure—the very thing we fear most—is actually a tool in the hand of God that heals, delivers, and sets us free. Do you remember how, when we were children, our moms told us that some cuts and scrapes would heal only if they were left uncovered and allowed fresh air? It is the same with emotional wounds. Such wounds heal only when they are uncovered and allowed to breathe. These issues are spiritual wounds, and they can be dealt with only by being exposed to the light of the Spirit of God.

When I speak of bringing issues into the light, I am not talking about confessing them to everyone in the church. I am talking about bringing them into the light of the Lord for healing. It would not have done any good for the woman with the issue of blood to tell her neighbors about her difficulty; they had no power to reverse her condition. The only place where we can find freedom from our issues is in the healing presence of our Lord. Exposing our issues and wounds to any other light but His is futile. The lesser lights of human compassion or human wisdom will not heal us. Jesus alone has the capability of healing our issues, because He alone...

was wounded for our transgressions, He [alone]
*was bruised for our iniquities; the chastisement for
our peace was upon Him, and* [only] *by His stripes
we are healed.*   (Isaiah 53:5 NKJV)

Entrusted

Issues must be entrusted to Jesus in order to be healed.
There is salvation in no other name under heaven than
that of Jesus Christ. It was only when the woman had
come to the end of her own resources and brought her
issue out into the light that she could receive healing.
And it was only by her reaching out to Jesus in total trust
that He was able to heal her.

This process requires total humility as well as total trust
that God is willing and able to heal us. The woman with
the issue of blood risked everything on her faith in the ability of Jesus to restore her. It will take no less from us if we
are to be whole. We must entrust ourselves into the hands
of Jesus as if we were helpless infants. In fact, we are totally
helpless outside of the grace of God through Jesus Christ.
All that we have and enjoy, we have because Jesus came to
give it to us. Jesus came so that we might experience life to
its utmost. He came to make us part of the Father's plan of
reconciliation of the world. He came so that we might be
one even as He and the Father are one.

Jesus also was sent to release captives. He was sent to
proclaim the favor of God, to bring those locked in darkness out into the light. Jesus Himself defined His ministry by reading the words of Isaiah:

*The Spirit of the Lord is upon me, because he hath
anointed me to preach the gospel to the poor; he*

> *hath sent me to heal the brokenhearted, to preach deliverance to the captives, and recovering of sight to the blind, to set at liberty them that are bruised, to preach the acceptable year of the Lord.*
>
> (Luke 4:18–19)

Issues that have been surrendered to the Lord will bring Him glory. If we could handle our own issues, who would get the glory? We would. But as we become exhausted, enlightened, and entrusted to Christ, it is He who gets the glory.

Are You Ready?

The woman with the issue of blood reached out to Christ from her defilement. Christ met her where she was, and He will meet you where you are. But you must take the step of faith. As the adage says, the journey of a thousand miles begins with one step. This is also true of your healing. Are you ready to take that step?

The woman also reached for Jesus out of desperation. Christ is the only source of true healing. The woman reached out to Jesus because she saw Christ as the only source of true life. Are you ready to lay everything else down? Are you desperate enough to be healed?

To minister effectively in the kingdom of God, we must rely on the grace of God rather than our own human abilities. God fills empty vessels with the oil of His grace. His strength is perfected in our weakness. You see, God gives us His strength to carry out His healing purpose. When divine power flowed out of Jesus into a powerless vessel, the result was healing. There was a

flow of power into this woman, just as there will be in us as we reach out to Jesus.

This book is for those who are tired of the segregation, the pain, the agony, the deprivation, and the exclusivity of their issue! It is for those who realize they have more to gain than to lose and are ready to make their private stuff public if necessary.

Throughout this book we will visit several of the issues with which many of us struggle—things like fear, shame, poverty, and pride. We will see how to deal with them by the grace of God and the truth of His Word, and find healing and wholeness together.

Are you ready to yield the secret things with which you wrestle? The things that keep you feeling defiled, unfruitful, separated, disqualified, and afraid? Are you ready to pinpoint the things that keep coming up over and over again to rob you of one opportunity after another? Have you said to yourself, *"I want to be used of God, but..."*?

Personal Reflections

Chapter Two

"...I'm Empty"

Chapter Two

"...I'm Empty"

The Issue of Emotional Need

There cometh a woman of Samaria to draw water....
—John 4:7

*I*t was a dry season in my life, a time when a void, an aching emptiness, something like pangs of hunger, was inside me. All that had been was ebbing away, and nothing seemed to be settled beneath my feet. I found myself wandering to a quiet place where I could be alone with my thoughts and my pain—a place that sheltered a very dark secret as well.

I was a married woman whose husband was ill—in fact, his medical prognosis was death. I watched him waste away physically, mentally, and even emotionally.

The powerful chemotherapy drugs, with their debilitating side effects, robbed him of his strength and vitality. Radiation treatments even stole the luster of his curly black hair. His ability as a great administrator and awesome minister eroded, along with his desire to live. Every now and then I would catch a glimpse of a twinkle in his eye, which reminded me of a former happier time. But now our conversation had become limited to, "How are you?" "What can I do for you to make you more comfortable?" and "Let's pray and sing, okay?" I felt alone and empty inside. I felt a deep thirst and a longing inside that troubled me in every conscious moment.

Then, in the midst of this driest of seasons, a secret issue erupted in my life. In my longing for the deep connection and sharing that I could no longer enjoy with my husband, I met a new friend—a new male friend. He was a man who loved God and my family, and he was a man who cared for me. It was so wonderful to enjoy meaningful conversation and laugh again, or just to sit together and ramble on about my family, my marriage, or my ministry. This friend became very special to me.

Not a day passed during which we didn't speak to one another in person or over the telephone. Whether he traveled in the country or abroad, I heard from him. What wonderful conversations we had. What prayers and encouragement we gave one another! I began to look forward to those times, and before long my day seemed to be incomplete if I didn't speak directly with my new friend.

Soon, however, a debate arose within me....

Is this man becoming too important? Am I thinking about him too often? I'm a married woman! Oh, what will I do if I miss his visit to my husband today? Should I call him or should I wait until he calls me? Oh, the disappointment I experience on the days that we don't speak.

God, help me. Am I falling in love with another man, or am I just appreciating what he has become in my life? I can't seem to think about anything or anyone else. God, I'm not just a wife and mother; I'm a minister, an executive pastor with responsibilities. What's happening to me?

My mind and my heart were in a whirl of confusion. I felt a mixture of joy and guilt. How could something that seemed to be so good trouble my thoughts so much? I needed wisdom. I sought a close Christian girlfriend for advice. She offered the thought that this new male friend might be God's way of providing a "bridge over troubled waters" for me. But somehow her words did not sit right with me. So I sought another source.

I went to my own daddy, who was a bishop and pastor, and asked him, "Daddy, would God give me permission to think about another man while I'm still married to a living husband?" Even as I asked the question, I was uncomfortable. Oh, Lord Jesus, this is becoming an issue. What should I do?

Finally I called my spiritual father, Bishop Reid. But when I asked Bishop Reid about this issue, he gave me no opinion. Instead he challenged me to inquire of the

Lord directly, to go beyond the wisdom of my family and friends to the Source of all wisdom.

When I finally asked the Lord, He brought to my mind another woman who lived in this same emptiness—another who had experienced this same deep thirst. He reminded me of the woman at the well in Sychar to whom Jesus spoke in the Gospel of John.

> *Then cometh he to a city of Samaria, which is called Sychar, near to the parcel of ground that Jacob gave to his son Joseph. Now Jacob's well was there. Jesus therefore, being wearied with his journey, sat thus on the well: and it was about the sixth hour. There cometh a woman of Samaria to draw water: Jesus saith unto her, Give me to drink.* (John 4:5–7)

As I read the passage, it was as if Jesus was speaking to me. This woman was my sister in heart. I could see her treading wearily over roads that had become as hot as burning coals in the heat of the midday sun. Her drab clothing hung loosely, and her veil, carelessly draped about her, outlined her worn and vacant face. This woman of Samaria was also one who was dry and thirsty, and she met Jesus at a place of refreshing, a place of cleansing water. She brought an empty vessel to Jacob's well to be filled, and filled it was—but not with any water that she expected.

As Jesus spoke with her, the woman discovered that Jesus knew of her emptiness and all the ways she had tried to satisfy it. Even though He knew all of her sinful ways, He did not censure her. Instead He opened her mind and her heart to know Him. Rather than punish

her, He offered her living water, a way out of her dryness. (And she wasn't even a Jew—she was a Samaritan.) With His healing, satisfying words, she became an evangelist, spreading the word of Jesus throughout her village.

As I treasured the words He spoke to me in this passage, a new song sprang from my heart. I knew that I could entrust my longing to Him. So I began to pour out my heart, telling Him things He already knew. My secret was not hidden from Him. He knew of my new friend, yet He called to me. He wooed me to Himself.

As I bared my heart to Jesus, a stream of praise began to well up within me and finally overflowed:

"I'm so thirsty for Your presence, Lord. I'm so thirsty for Your love, Your compassion, Your affirmation. I'm so thirsty to know You more. I'm thirsty to experience Your power again! Lord, *give me this water, that I thirst not, neither come hither to draw'* (John 4:15)."

He did not crush me, punish me, or worse, ignore me. He did not call to me to reject me; He was spirit, life, and truth to me, and so much more! I could expose all that was in my heart and worship Him *"in spirit and in truth"* (v. 23). He did not send His Spirit to condemn me, but to confront me and draw me back to the Source of all living waters. It was His Spirit that had caused the unsettledness in my heart until I found Him beside the well at Sychar.

"I am empty, famished in body and soul. With an empty vessel on my shoulder, I set out to find You. I have

been so caught up with carnal needs that I have ignored my soul. But today I can't dismiss the yearnings and cravings for something higher and better—something that quenches this deep thirst. Only You, Lord; I want only You. I want to run to You, Jesus. I'm tired, weary, frustrated. My whole being aches for that deep, living water."

Offer a Drink of Praise

Although I had at first slipped into His presence with my own worldly agenda, I heard His voice say to me, *"Give me to drink...."* He, too, had a thirst to be satisfied, and the only thing that He had to draw with was *me!* I had approached Him, shy, frightened, and alone, with a dark and awful secret. But before I could speak, He drew praise from the depths of my heart. Praise displaced the gnawing emptiness of my longing as I began to minister to the Lord.

"Yes, I praise You, Lord, as the married woman with another man on her mind! I praise You, Lord, as the minister who has run from the prayer closet for the past two days. I praise You, Lord, as the hurting, angry, embittered wife. I praise You, Lord!"

I was as amazed as that Samaritan woman must have been. Can the Lord use me despite this emptiness, despite the natural desire that had so seized my heart? Yes! This gnawing emptiness was the very thing that the Lord had used to draw me to Himself. Just as that woman came to a natural spring and found spiritual water, so Jesus gave me a drink from His well of living water.

Whosoever drinketh of the water that I shall give him shall never thirst; but the water that I shall give him shall be in him a well of water springing up into everlasting life. (John 4:14)

I was transported to a new level of life. Jesus knew all that was in my heart, including my "friend." His response to my thirst inspired an even greater longing in my heart. I prayed, "Give me this water, Lord!"

If was as if He said to me, "There is only One who can satisfy your emptiness, and *'I that speak unto thee am he'* (v. 26)." This once weary, broken woman found true healing for her longing. And like the woman at the well, I left my waterpot that holds only natural water, natural comforts, and declare to you as she did, *"Come, see a man, which told me all things that ever I did: is not this the Christ?"* (v. 29).

Settling the Issue of Emptiness

As I stood before the Lord in my old jogging suit, I was inspired to praise and worship Him despite my circumstances and secrets. As I knelt and opened my mouth to praise and extol who Jesus had become and what He meant to me personally, I was suddenly caught up in the Spirit—lifted above my issues, my secrets, and taken into His sweet arms. As I told Him about my husband and his condition, He silenced me. As I thought of the relationship with my new male friend, He spoke a deep hush over my soul that reached to the very source of my issue of emptiness. Jesus reached out and touched me, gently confronting me with the knowledge that

nothing—absolutely nothing—in my life was hidden from Him.

And, as He always does, the Lord gave me a clear way out of the carnal issue that had captivated my emotions. He told me that from that day on, I was not to initiate conversations with my friend. I was not to be available when he came to visit my husband. I was not to call him at his office, residence, or on his cell phone. The very moment I agreed to obey His word to me, I was relieved of my guilt and shame. His truth brought deliverance and set my aching heart free!

It was not some stern rebuke or threat of punishment that allowed me to turn toward the Lord. It was His presence, His kindness, that wrested me from my own efforts to fill the emptiness and turned me back to the true Source of satisfaction. My issue was brought into the open, and I heard His voice and responded to His invitation. I repented, and He immediately restored me. I rose from my worship that day consecrated and rededicated to ministry and the covenant of marriage "till death do us part."

What a comfort it is to know that there is a Fountain of living water that can eternally refresh all those who are parched by the issues of secret sins and sufferings. How delightful to realize that Jesus the Christ comes to show us the inner meaning of worship! We can come to drink of the Water of Life freely—not the water in the well of Sychar, but the spiritual refreshment we receive when we encounter and are touched by Jesus. *Even with my issue* of emptiness, I was drawn to worship at the throne of God. It was Jesus whom I had thirsted for all along, and

it was only Jesus who could fill me with new life and a
new peace. He did not use me despite my issue; He used
me because of it.

> *They shall not hunger nor thirst; neither shall the
> heat nor sun smite them: for he that hath mercy on
> them shall lead them, even by the springs of water
> shall he guide them.* (Isaiah 49:10)

> *But whosoever drinketh of the water that I shall
> give him shall never thirst; but the water that I shall
> give him shall be in him a well of water springing
> up into everlasting life.* (John 4:14)

Personal Reflections

Chapter Three

"...I'm a Ciar"

Chapter Three

"...I'm a Liar"

The Issue of Integrity

Let no corrupt communication proceed out of your mouth, but that which is good to the use of edifying, that it may minister grace unto the hearers.
—*Ephesians 4:29*

I was a young freshman in college, slumped uncomfortably in a chair opposite my senior pastor, Bishop Frank Bowden. It was a time of prayer and fasting prior to Easter, when anyone in the congregation was encouraged to make a ten-minute appointment with our busy senior pastor to pray about the areas in our lives where we were challenged or convicted. My pastor had preached a message from Psalm 101 that said, *"He that worketh deceit*

shall not dwell within my house: he that telleth lies shall not tarry in my sight" (v. 7). His message spoke to my heart, telling me that anyone who lies would not be welcomed into the presence of God; he or she would be rejected. *Rejected!* I hated the feeling of that word.

I was the third of thirteen children, and I had learned to shade and manipulate the truth in order to avoid punishment, at least for a while. I could get lost in the crowd, so to speak. I guess that lying became a way to maintain my acceptance in the family. But now, to my horror, I realized that rejection—the very thing I was trying to avoid—could become the consequence of my lying lifestyle. I could not stand the thought of being rejected by God, so I made an appointment with Bishop Bowden to come clean.

My face was flushed as I stumbled over my words, fighting the urge to leave rather than reveal the secret I had carried all my life. But I gulped and forced myself to continue. "Sir, thank you for the faith and trust you have invested in me, allowing me to serve in your music department. But I've got a problem—an issue—and I can't keep it to myself any longer! You see, although I always try really hard to tell the truth, I find myself, well, lying—stretching the truth—and I know it's wrong. Since Sunday school classes as a little girl, I have been taught that Jesus is *'the way, the truth, and the life'* (John 14:6). I know and love Jesus so very much. And yet, even though I know better, sometimes it's just easier for me to lie. Sometimes I'll just be laughing and sharing a story, and before I know it, the story line changes. To get a laugh, or acceptance, or approval or affirmation, I hear myself stretching the truth. Bishop, you spoke that 'liars

shall not tarry in the sight of God.' I realize now that *I am a liar,* and I don't want to be separated from God. Please help me! Maybe you can ask God to stop me from talking so much, and then I wouldn't have the opportunity to lie! Help me, please."

Bishop Bowden looked warmly into my eyes and spoke to my issue, "Daughter, I commend your desire to confront this major issue at your age. I remind you this month, as we celebrate the death and resurrection of our Lord Jesus Christ, that it was for you that Jesus died. 'He was hung up for your hang-ups.' He rose again to give you grace to deal with all of the issues that you will encounter in your life. He doesn't want you to stop talking; rather, He wants you to speak words of value and purpose that will point people to Him. If you are ready to exchange speaking lies for speaking truth, then I am ready to pray with and for you."

After an awesome yet comforting prayer, I lifted my head to accept the real truth of the matter: I was now responsible for replacing lies with truth. I had to take steps—big steps, in fact—to ensure that I walked in truth and nothing but the truth, so help me God.

My minister counseled me that whenever I found myself stretching the truth, I was to immediately identify that I had lied. He called it "shining light on darkness." I had an immediate opportunity to practice his counsel. Sitting around the student union hall at Chapman College, a lie slipped out, but I immediately corrected it. A few days of this actually put a stop to it completely. With God's help, I am still able to put a stop to the issue of lying by exposing falsehoods and half-truths

the moment they are spoken. Is it easy? No! Is it necessary in order for me to achieve and succeed? Yes!

What really happened that day in the midst of the pastoral counseling session that changed my life forever? Did my minister condemn me to hell? Did he fire me on the spot from my position as organist? Did he remove me or disqualify me from serving the Lord? No! He pointed me to a power greater than myself, One who could direct me, forgive me, and then challenge me as never before: the Lord Jesus Christ.

Somehow God was able to use me in service to Him even when I was a liar. You may ask, "How does God use a liar?" Any way He wants! Our gifts, ministries, and blessings come from God. They are not just natural abilities; they are blessings that flow through us into the world. The truth is that God uses imperfect people because that's the only kind He has.

God's Plan Is Bigger than People

God used another famous liar and deceiver in the Bible: Jacob. Jacob and his mother, Rebekah, conspired to steal a blessing from Jacob's brother Esau. Jacob took advantage of his own brother's weakness and tricked him out of his birthright. Esau, the elder brother, had grown up to be a real man's man. He liked to be out in the fields hunting and providing for the family. Jacob, on the other hand, was a *"plain man"* (Genesis 25:27); in other words, he did not stand out in the crowd. We sort of get the idea that Jacob hung around the camp looking for opportunity. And one day Esau came in from being in

the field, weak with hunger. Seeing an opportunity, Jacob offered him a pot of lentil soup in exchange for Esau's birthright. As with all who are carnally minded, Esau handed over an eternal treasure for a momentary desire. (See Genesis 25:27–34.)

A little while later, Rebekah was eavesdropping on her husband, Isaac, and overheard that he was about to hand over the blessings and the reins to Esau, and rightfully so, because he was the firstborn. But Rebekah had her own plans and preferences. She devised a scheme to route the blessing and all that it conveyed to her favorite son, Jacob. She disguised Jacob to look and smell like his brother Esau in the blind eyes of their father Isaac. Isaac fell for the plan, and the blessing was given to Jacob. Essentially, Jacob and Rebekah stole Esau's identity and blessing by lying. (See Genesis 27:1–29.) If anyone was undeserving of blessing, it was Jacob, whose very name reeks of crookedness and deception. Yet he was blessed, and Isaac, his father, could not take back the blessing. How can this be? How can God use a liar?

When Rebekah was pregnant with her sons, God spoke a word of prophecy concerning them both. He said,

Two nations are in thy womb, and two manner of people shall be separated from thy bowels; and the one people shall be stronger than the other people; and the elder shall serve the younger.
(Genesis 25:23)

God had a plan that was much bigger than one liar, and He still does. The blessing that was passed on to Jacob, even by deception, had originated in God and was

given to Abraham, then passed from Abraham to Isaac, and from Isaac to Jacob. That blessing would be passed on through Jacob to his own grandchildren, who became the nation of Israel. Then that same blessing, though tainted by deception, was passed on to us through Jesus Christ.

God gives us gifts and abilities to be used, and He does not take them back because we make mistakes. *"For the gifts and calling of God are without repentance"* (Romans 11:29). That is how God could still use me, or anyone else, even though I was not always truthful.

The lineage of Jesus is dotted with many imperfect people. The list in Luke 3:23–38 includes liars, prostitutes, murderers, and other less-than-perfect people. But they were all people whom God used in some powerful ways, and the blessing of God passed through them. Rahab, a harlot, saved her family and married into the family of Israel. Ruth was a Moabitess, a pagan, but she became the wife of Boaz and the grandmother of David. David plotted the murder of the husband of a woman with whom he committed adultery, yet the most enduring words of praise in all of history flowed out of him—because of God's grace and worthiness, not David's.

Jacob did not get away with his deception, because God had a plan for that as well. Jacob was driven out of the camp of his family and into the wilderness, and eventually he landed destitute in the home of his lying and conniving uncle Laban. For years he was surrounded by deception, including being tricked out of marrying the love of his life and being taken advantage of to increase Laban's wealth.

Settling the Issue of Lying

Why do we lie? Well, we could blame it all on the devil, who is the "father of lies." (See John 8:44.) But in reality, lies originate from a fear of rejection or of harm of some kind. When I was a little girl, I lied to avoid being rejected (punished) by my parents. When I got older, I lied to be accepted by peers.

Lying is the oldest sin in the Book. Satan lied to Adam and Eve, and Adam continued the lie by trying to blame Eve for his own sin instead of facing up to the consequences. The family fibbing continued when Cain lied about his brother Abel, whom he had murdered. So the issue of lying is generational as well. Abram was bitten by the same bug, too. No sooner had Abram received the blessings and promises of God when he lied to protect himself. Faced with possible danger from the king of Egypt, Abram lied and said that his wife Sarai was his sister. (See Genesis 12:11–19.) When faced with the same threat, Abram's son Isaac also lied about his own wife. (See Genesis 26:7.) Is it any wonder that it was passed to Jacob?

The Bible mentions many others who told lies, including Peter. (See Matthew 26:69–70.) Peter lied about being associated with Jesus in order to avoid danger. Still, despite Peter's lying ways, Jesus entrusted him with His own flock. The very one who denied Jesus was given a place of authority as shepherd of the Jerusalem Church.

So when they had dined, Jesus saith to Simon Peter, Simon, son of Jonas, lovest thou me more than these? He saith unto him, Yea, Lord; thou knowest

that I love thee. He saith unto him, Feed my lambs. He saith to him again the second time, Simon, son of Jonas, lovest thou me? He saith unto him, Yea, Lord; thou knowest that I love thee. He saith unto him, Feed my sheep. He saith unto him the third time, Simon, son of Jonas, lovest thou me? Peter was grieved because he said unto him the third time, Lovest thou me? And he said unto him, Lord, thou knowest all things; thou knowest that I love thee. Jesus saith unto him, Feed my sheep.

(John 21:15–17)

Note the restoring heart of God. Peter had denied Jesus three times at a *"fire of coals"* (John 18:18) in the palace, and it was at another *"fire of coals"* (John 21:9) on the seashore where Jesus restored Peter three times. Later it was this same Peter, the liar, who gave the fiery sermon at the temple that converted thousands in an afternoon. (See Acts 2:14–36.) It was this same Peter who was the first to baptize Gentiles at the home of Cornelius. God used Peter in all of these instances, not because Peter was worthy, but because he was repentant and usable in God's hands.

Now, many years after dealing with my issue of lying, the Lord has restored me and used me as a teacher, an evangelist, a counselor, a musician, an administrator, and a trustee of the most awesome truth, the Word of God. He did so not because of my worthiness, but because of His purpose and grace. And God will use you as well, as you surrender to Him and speak the truth.

If we are to settle the issue of lying, then we must first realize that God is trustworthy. At the root of our

untruthfulness is a mistrust of God. Adam lied because he did not trust God to forgive him. Abraham lied because he did not trust God to protect him. Peter lied because he did not trust that God was in control of the situation concerning Jesus. Whenever you and I tell a lie, it is because at some level we do not trust that we have been accepted by God and so proceed to seek the approval of others.

But God our Father is faithful!

> *Be strong and of a good courage, fear not, nor be afraid of them: for the LORD thy God, he it is that doth go with thee; he will not fail thee, nor forsake thee.* (Deuteronomy 31:6)

God always has our best in mind. God will always accomplish His purpose where we are concerned. Whatever God speaks, God will do. We have no reason to fear. And He will even use imperfect people like you and me.

> *Faithful is he that calleth you, who also will do it.* (1 Thessalonians 5:24)

Pray with me:

> O precious and faithful Father God, I confess to You that I have not always trusted You enough to tell the truth. I have tried to impress others and gain approval by false means. I know that You desire truth in the inward parts (Psalm 51:6), and I ask You to cleanse me now by the blood of Christ and replace lies with the truth. I ask that by Your enabling grace You will help me to speak the truth and bring glory to Your name forever. Amen.

Personal Reflections

Chapter Four

"...I'm Proud"

Chapter Four

"...I'm Proud"

The Issue of Pride

His name was Robert. He was a man who had achieved a high position in his career, and who was well liked and respected. Whenever a great challenge or crisis situation arose, people called for Robert. Aside from his great natural abilities, Robert had a dynamic and engaging personality. He could talk to anyone about anything, and he always seemed to be confident regardless of the situation in which he found himself. A gifted leader, he was successful in all that he did. He had wealth, a wonderful family, servants, and nowhere to go but up. Everything seemed to be going his way—except for the fact that he had AIDS. In the prime

of his life, he got infected with the HIV virus during a medical procedure. So, although he was handsome, wealthy, influential, and successful, he was as good as dead. His condition would kill him inch by inch over a long and agonizing period of time.

Robert...can you picture him? He's really a contemporary version of "Naaman," the captain of Syria's army.

> *Now Naaman, captain of the host of the king of Syria, was a great man with his master, and honourable, because by him the LORD had given deliverance unto Syria: he was also a mighty man in valour, but he was a leper.* (2 Kings 5:1)

Naaman was an impressive man by all accounts, with all the credentials we mentioned above. However, he had one more thing that made all the other things worthless: the issue of pride.

Naaman was the successful commander-in-chief of Syria's army; he had received many military honors and had known much good fortune. But this wealthy, successful military personality had a problem that preempted all of his accomplishments. He was a leper. This disease was the AIDS of his day. It was for the most part incurable, painful, and eventually terminal.

In the nation of Israel, a person infected with leprosy was set apart for seven days to be observed by the priests. If the symptoms did not go away, the infected person would have to leave the love and security of his family and live outside the camp (or city) in total separation. Lepers were separated so that they would not infect others and bring danger to the rest of the camp. The books of the

Law provided the guidelines for the treatment of people with leprosy; the instructions were quite clear.

> *Command the children of Israel, that they put out of the camp every leper.* (Numbers 5:2)

However, Naaman was not of Israel, but Syria, which had no such law regarding leprosy. So even with his leprous condition Naaman was not excluded from other people. Instead, he was allowed to continue in his position. Nonetheless, he must have been a pitiful sight. Imagine this man of great power and stature who could not wear the robes and emblems of his office because of festering ulcers and the rotten flesh that clung to him. In the midst of Naaman's wretchedness, though, the God of Israel had pity on him.

Biblical record has it that Naaman's wife had an Israelite maidservant who had been captured in a border skirmish between Syria and Israel. It was this nameless maid residing in their home who would be used to usher this man into great healing and rebirth. Her sympathy for Naaman's condition moved her to speak to his wife, saying, *"Would God my lord were with the prophet that is in Samaria! for he would recover him of his leprosy"* (2 Kings 5:3). Through the word of a servant, God would bring healing not only of leprosy, but also of Naaman's chief issue, which was pride. Naaman would be brought to the knowledge of God.

So here came Naaman, the great commander of the Syrian host. He and a large company of brave warriors riding on white horses and in chariots arrived at the door of Elisha, the prophet of God. The display was a blend

of power and pity. But instead of being invited into the prophet's house, he was snubbed at the door by a lowly servant timidly telling him to go and wash in the Jordan River, dipping himself not once, but seven times!

That was it! He had had enough of this degradation and insolence. Here he was being told to wash in a muddy little river by a slave, to whom he had been sent by the pity of a captured maidservant. Pitied! Snubbed! Insulted! Furious! (See 2 Kings 5:4–12.) This was ridiculous! "I thought he would come out to me, and that he would wave his hand and heal me," said the disgruntled warrior. Couldn't he wash in the grand and golden rivers of his homeland? Why must he wash in this insignificant tributary? It was all too humiliating. He grabbed the reins of his horse in anger and prepared to turn his back on the healing of God. Why? All because he was afraid it would make him look bad. This brave and fearless warrior was led to the very door of healing, but he chose to turn and walk away simply because of pride.

The Problem with Pride

How many of us recognize, regardless of our self-image, that pride can prevent our progress and success in life? Pride stops us and turns us away from the door of healing and intimacy with God. In pride, we stumble and trip over our own egos.

What is pride? Pride is an attitude that allows us a high opinion of our abilities or ourselves. Pride is the belief that we are somehow above other people. As the Bible says, *"Pride goeth before destruction, and an haughty*

spirit before a fall" (Proverbs 16:18). Pride is the opposite of humility. Humility is our awareness of who we are as we focus on God; pride is our awareness of who we are as we focus on ourselves.

The Hebrew word for pride comes from the thought of being lifted up above the rest. I can almost see Naaman sitting on his tall white horse looking down with disdain on those to whom he was led. The problem is that when we spend so much time with our heads lifted up in pride, we fail to notice the little obstacles under our feet that make us stumble. Pride carries with it the fear of falling below the image we wish to convey to other people. Pride makes us more concerned about our reputation than our character.

It was pride that turned lucifer away from God to worship himself, as we read in Ezekiel:

> *Son of man, say unto the prince of Tyrus, Thus saith the Lord GOD; Because thine heart is lifted up, and thou hast said, I am a God, I sit in the seat of God, in the midst of the seas; yet thou art a man, and not God, though thou set thine heart as the heart of God.* (Ezekiel 28:2)

The prince of Tyre in this passage represents lucifer, who fell away from God in his own arrogant self-worship. It was pride that separated lucifer from the presence of God, just as pride almost separated Naaman from his healing.

Of course, the Bible is not comparing pride to leprosy in the story of Naaman. Pride was the issue that almost kept Naaman from being healed of leprosy. Spiritually

speaking, leprosy is the carnality that we so often live in. So what must be healed is the pride that keeps us living in our own carnal strength. Without this healing, we die an inch at a time.

Events in the life of my own late husband brought home to me the dangers of pride. While ministering alone in Haiti on a mission trip, my husband became very ill. His strength was leaving him, and his skin had broken out all over his body. He was suffering from fevers, chills, and sleepless nights. But in all this he refused to seek medical attention.

By the mercy of God, an American woman spotted him sitting in a medical office having difficulty breathing. When she learned that he was from the United States, she got his home number and called me. Because of the political unrest and questionable medical facilities in Haiti, she advised me not to seek medical attention for my husband there. Rather, he needed to come home fast. She said that if we would purchase first-class tickets for them both, she would accompany him back to the States.

There was no debate as to what we needed to do. We would get those tickets regardless of the cost. So I purchased two first-class tickets and went to Philadelphia to meet the flight. I waited anxiously at the Philadelphia International Airport. After all the other passengers and crew had left the aircraft, two final passengers appeared at the door. One was the woman I had spoken with, and the other was a sickly, frail man with an oxygen mask over his face. *Oh, my God, that can't be him,* I thought to myself. But it was my husband. This powerful preacher of

the Word, this man who seemed invincible, had become ill almost beyond my recognition.

The very warm and friendly woman who had accompanied my husband threw her arms around me and said in a tone of relief, "We made it!" She advised me that my husband needed medical attention right away. He refused, stating that all he needed was some rest and he would be fine. I silently wept as I wheeled him to the waiting car and drove to the hotel where we were to stay overnight before continuing the journey back home. Once there, he was advised again to see a doctor. He said, "No way!" What was I to do? I did what you do most when faced with such an issue—pray!

As I prayed, I sensed that I was simply to step back and wait for change. And change came—in the middle of the night, when my husband woke up choking and panting for air to breathe. Without hesitation, he pushed out the words, "Get a doctor." How awesomely God will work once we push past fear and pride! When I called the front desk of the hotel for assistance, they told me that one of the country's top pulmonary specialists lived in the penthouse. Within minutes, a knock on our hotel door gave entrance to a man whom I soon called "my angel." This skilled doctor examined my husband and immediately called for an ambulance to take him to the hospital. If we had not gotten him medical treatment, his life would have been measured in hours. He was sick unto death. My husband ultimately did pass away from this condition, but his life was extended for years because the Lord humbled him to seek medical attention.

Pride is absolutely destructive. Pride robs us of blessing and intimacy with God and leaves us busted, disgusted, and maladjusted. If we are to move on in God and experience His power, then we must deal with the issue of pride.

Settling the Issue of Pride

What is the source of issues of pride? Perhaps they come from a kind of spiritual amnesia; we forget who God is. We forget who has delivered us from the bondage of sin. We forget who has supplied and blessed us beyond measure. We forget that our total purpose is to love and glorify God. It is dangerous to forget. God warned the people of Israel about what happens when they forget Him and become lifted up in pride. (Read Deuteronomy 8:11–19.)

When we forget that we live by the grace of God, we try to live in our own strength. It was God who told Israel that they would live in houses they did not build and eat from vines they did not plant. Did you ever ask God for something that you really needed or wanted, and then when you got it you forgot who gave it to you? Somehow we tend to forget God and begin to live in our own strength. It is those places where we forget about God in our lives that become sources of pride in us. We have even seen ministers of the Gospel begin to be lifted up in pride because they forgot that they stood before the people of God by virtue of a blood-drenched cross. When we forget God, we become lifted up in pride.

When we are in pride, we try to go life alone. Pride keeps us from hearing and heeding the Word of

God. We cannot accept counsel and grace from others. However, there are some issues in our lives in which God will send a man or woman to assist us. No matter how great and important we think we are, there are some things in which we need the help of others in the body of Christ.

Naaman's unnamed servants seem to have had a good grasp on the truth. Note how the servants got to the heart of the issue of pride.

> *And his servants came near, and spake unto him, and said, My father, if the prophet had bid thee do some great thing, wouldest thou not have done it? how much rather then, when he saith to thee, Wash, and be clean?* (2 Kings 5:13)

If the man of God had asked Naaman to do something great, like kill a giant, then Naaman would gladly have done so. Why? Because that would have made Naaman the one who secured his own healing. If the prophet had asked Naaman to win some great military victory in order to earn a healing, Naaman would have done it and felt good about it. Again, Naaman would not have had to trust God for healing, but only in his own abilities.

Besides pride being the result of forgetting God, it also stems from not trusting God and instead relying upon ourselves. When we achieve something through our own natural means, we tend to paint God out of the picture. Yes, we may be great teachers or we may sing well, but in whom did those gifts originate? God! So, even though Naaman was a mighty warrior and the captain of an army, he still had to rely upon the mercy of God.

Naaman was able to hear the truth of his servants' words.

> *Then went he down, and dipped himself seven times in Jordan, according to the saying of the man of God: and his flesh came again like unto the flesh of a little child, and he was clean.*   (2 Kings 5:14)

Naaman was healed and reborn at the same time. The Bible says that he came up from the waters of the Jordan with flesh like a little child's. Thus he was healed not only from leprosy, but also from the issue of pride. Naaman submitted himself to the true and living God and was healed by His grace alone. How often we, too, become prideful when we forget that we are saved by grace alone simply by trusting God!

> *For by grace are ye saved through faith; and that not of yourselves: it is the gift of God: not of works, lest any man should boast.*   (Ephesians 2:8–9)

Healed of the issue of pride, Naaman returned to praise the Lord, saying, *"Behold, now I know that there is no God in all earth, but in Israel"* (2 Kings 5:15). Is this our declaration as well? Do we place our trust in anything or anyone but the Lord Himself? Have we forgotten who we are and whose we are? If we are to settle the issue of pride, it will be by remembering and trusting the Lord alone.

All of us struggle with the issue of pride to some degree at some time. Let's read and then pray through this Scripture to remind ourselves that God is the source of all that we have and all that we are.

And it shall be, when the LORD thy God shall have brought thee into the land which he sware unto thy fathers, to Abraham, to Isaac, and to Jacob, to give thee great and goodly cities, which thou buildedst not, and houses full of all good things, which thou filledst not, and wells digged, which thou diggedst not, vineyards and olive trees, which thou plantedst not; when thou shalt have eaten and be full; then beware lest thou forget the LORD, which brought thee forth out of the land of Egypt, from the house of bondage. (Deuteronomy 6:10–12)

Lord, I remind myself that it was You who brought me out of the bondage of sin. I remind myself that all that I have comes from Your hand alone. I remind myself that all of my gifts and abilities have their source in You, and that the anointing that runs over me flows from Your own vineyard. Lord, I remind myself that my very life came from Your breath. As I live in Your presence I ask that I never forget You. Heal me and cleanse me from any area of pride—any area where I have forgotten You. I thank You in Jesus' name. Amen.

Personal Reflections

Chapter Five

"...I'm Afraid"

Chapter Five

"...I'm Afraid"

The Issue of Fear

Be not afraid, only believe.
—Mark 5:36

Something was terribly wrong. I was getting weaker by the day, and I was so tired that all I wanted to do was go to bed and sleep forever. *Lord, what's wrong with me?*

At first I thought that I had simply gone back to work too soon after the birth of my daughter; perhaps six weeks had not been enough time to recover. But my husband was in school, and we needed the income. Then I thought that perhaps I was just worn out, but nine months later I was still feeling sick and tired. I was so

pale that one of my friends suggested I might be anemic. I didn't know what was happening to me, so I scheduled an appointment with my personal physician.

Then, one day before my appointment with my doctor, I began to feel faint as I sat at my desk. The world began to spin, and suddenly everything went black. The next thing I knew, I was on the floor drifting in and out of consciousness. I wasn't sure if I had passed out or not. I was aware of someone moving me, and somehow I was taken to the hospital. I was hemorrhaging and didn't know it. All I could think about was that someone needed to find my husband, call my mother, and pray. *Lord, what is happening to me?*

I sat stunned sometime later when my doctor told me that I needed major surgery. At first they tried a minor surgical procedure and medication, but neither was able to stop the bleeding. A pathologist's report revealed that I had cancer, and it was in the third stage. I was going to need a total hysterectomy. Surely there was some mistake…my doctor had to be talking about someone else. I was only twenty-three years old. How could this be happening to me? *Not me, Lord. My youngest child is just ten months old, and my oldest child is three. Lord, what about the son we wanted so badly? This procedure means no more children. What should I do?*

I began to bargain with myself. I reasoned that if I could go to church and have my pastor pray for me, maybe the Lord would just heal me and this would all go away supernaturally. Then I wouldn't have to worry about surgery or any other medical procedure. As I sat

quietly in the Sunday Worship Celebration, a woman slipped into the seat beside me and whispered in my ear, "God can do it without a knife or doctor. Where is your faith?" Her words only served to add guilt to my pain. *Did I trust the Lord? Should I cancel the surgery? What should I do?*

Is God Delayed?

There is no greater thrill than seeing the power of God moving in some supernatural way. We are in awe when we see someone climb out of a wheelchair or find freedom from the bondage of sin. When those miraculous moments come, praise erupts from our hearts into the heavens. It's easy to give glory to God and to shout hallelujah when He moves on our behalf in response to our desperate need. But what of those times when we prayed and besought God without obvious result? What do we do in those times when we really need God to move in healing or provision on our behalf, but He seems to be busy with something more important? Was there ever a day in your life when you prayed and told God that you needed that check to arrive in the mail *today,* and it didn't? Have you ever experienced a season when you needed a word from God, but your prayers rebounded off a brassy heaven? Have you ever stayed up all night with a sick child, begging God for a touch of His hand? Yes, I think we all have seen those days and seasons. And it is how we respond in these times of seeming delay that demonstrates how well we know God.

We in today's society have become accustomed to instant solutions for everything. Family times around the

table have been replaced by microwave meals eaten on the run to the next activity. Computerized counselors dispense volumes of information in nanoseconds, giving us instant answers. When it comes to God, our problem is that we expect Him to be our cosmic Internet server from which we can download help for our every dilemma. And if God does not come through with instant relief, we begin to question our "connection" to heaven.

When we have to wait on God, it seems as though a chasm forms between our need and His compassion—a gulf filled with agony and apathy. As we stand at the rim of this canyon, our hearts respond with either fear or faith, depending on what we believe about God. If we believe God to be loving and involved, then we will tend toward faith. But if we believe God to be far off and removed, then we will be afraid.

There is probably no greater agony in waiting than when we are waiting for the Lord to move on behalf of our children. When children are sick, both they and those who care for them feel helpless. When a child runs a fever in the middle of the night, all we can do is wait and pray that the remedy we've applied will take effect. Imagine what it must have been like two thousand years ago when even things like aspirin were unknown and unavailable. Children still got sick, and many of them died from things that seem trivial today.

Such was the dire circumstance of Jairus, the president or the ruler of the synagogue, and his only daughter, who are mentioned in the Gospels. Jairus had a need that his spiritual, political, economic, and social influence could

not fill. In this time of great need, Jairus was moved from great fear to greater faith.

> And, behold, there cometh one of the rulers of the synagogue, Jairus by name; and when he saw him, he fell at his feet, and besought him greatly, saying, My little daughter lieth at the point of death: I pray thee, come and lay thy hands on her, that she may be healed; and she shall live. And Jesus went with him; and much people followed him, and thronged him....While he yet spake, there came from the ruler of the synagogue's house certain which said, Thy daughter is dead: why troublest thou the Master any further? As soon as Jesus heard the word that was spoken, he saith unto the ruler of the synagogue, Be not afraid, only believe. And he suffered no man to follow him, save Peter, and James, and John the brother of James. And he cometh to the house of the ruler of the synagogue, and seeth the tumult, and them that wept and wailed greatly. And when he was come in, he saith unto them, Why make ye this ado, and weep? the damsel is not dead, but sleepeth. And they laughed him to scorn. But when he had put them all out, he taketh the father and the mother of the damsel, and them that were with him, and entereth in where the damsel was lying. And he took the damsel by the hand, and said unto her, Talitha cumi; which is, being interpreted, Damsel, I say unto thee, arise. And straightway the damsel arose, and walked; for she was of the age of twelve years. And they were astonished with a great astonishment. And he charged them straitly that no man should know it; and commanded that something should be given her to eat.   (Mark 5:22–24; 35–43)

The Issue of Fear

Jairus had heard Jesus teach many times. Indeed, as ruler of the synagogue, it was Jairus who gave Jesus opportunity to speak. And when Jesus spoke, musty old scrolls came to life, their words becoming more than the ritual recitation to which the people had grown accustomed. In the background, jeers and complaints from Jairus' fellow Pharisees picked apart and distorted the words of the Master. Some of them even said that Jesus Himself had demons. But despite all of this, Jairus saw something in Jesus that rose above all of the academic and religious banter. There was a growing awareness in Jairus' heart that the warmth and compassion of God were resident within Jesus.

Now the young daughter of Jairus lay sick with an unnamed illness, perhaps unto death. Her appetite was gone and her speech reduced to occasional whimpers. Jairus and his wife had witnessed this scene played out hundreds of times in the surrounding village: the death of children to the most minor of infections or childhood diseases. They could only stand by and watch the blush of her youth disappear as the final embers of her life grew dimmer with each passing day. These were desperate times that called for desperate measures. But what measures?

The answer seemed plain to Jairus as he watched his daughter fade with each labored breath. There was only one hope of saving this one whom he loved: Jesus. He had seen Jesus straighten crooked limbs and open blind eyes with an utterance. He had seen Jesus correct all

manner of sickness under His gentle hands. Why not this little one? This father would give all, risk all, to save his daughter, and turn a blind eye to any who might question his action. So Jairus set out to join the throng of those who greeted the returning Jesus.

The crowd was thick with need, but somehow Jairus was able to break through to Jesus. As he stood before the Lord, Jairus was overcome by the urgency of his need and collapsed at Jesus' feet. Then, looking up into those dark Hebrew eyes of Jesus, he said, "Jesus, Master, my little girl is dying. If You would just come to my home and touch her, I believe that she will be healed and live!" Without so much as a word, Jesus motioned to Jairus to lead the way to his daughter. The tide and current of the throng changed direction and fell in behind Jesus as He set out toward the home of Jairus.

Jairus was ecstatic. He kept looking back over his shoulder to make sure that Jesus was still there. Hope flooded the heart of Jairus as he thought, *Help is on the way. My little girl will live.* Jairus now walked along at a quicker pace, reinvigorated at the prospect of healing. Then, suddenly, a woman's hand shot out of the crowd and laid hold of the Master's garment. Jesus stopped. The disciples stopped. Everyone stopped. What was happening? Jesus spoke no word. There was only a sudden pivot and change of direction—away from Jairus' home and the healing of his daughter.

Now Jesus was focused on a woman dressed in tattered clothing who seemed to be tearfully muttering something at His feet. Jesus stood with His back turned

to Jairus to address some unknown woman. *What is He saying? What could be more important than my little girl?* Panic set in upon Jairus as this unexpected "hand" delayed the procession. His daughter's healing was slipping away, and he could only stand and wait for the Master to move in his direction again. His heart, once filled with the hope and vision of healing, was now heavy with fear that it was just not his time—fear that his only daughter would not last until Jesus could get to her.

Then, just as Jesus was speaking a final word to the woman, some men walked hurriedly up behind Jairus, calling out his name. Jairus spun around, now with his back toward Jesus, to hear the crushing news that it was too late. His daughter was dead. Stunned, Jairus' face went flush with shock. He stood dazed and numb, drawing shallow breaths, his worst fears realized.

All the while Jesus stood listening to the report, still speaking no word to Jairus. But then, into the fear and hopelessness that were written all over the man's face, Jesus opened His mouth and said, "Don't be afraid; trust Me." Jesus' words were spoken in firm but personal tones. He wasn't preaching to Jairus; He was encouraging him. The time of delay was only in the mind of an anxious father. In his mind, the urgency of the need had overshadowed the heart and intention of God. But God was aware of both the need and the unsettled heart of the father, and He would bring peace to both.

Jesus now chose three, Peter, James, and John, who would witness His reign over life and death, and continued toward the home of Jairus. The group arrived to hear the

sounds of mourning filling the streets around the house. Then Jesus, along with the parents of the little girl and the three witnesses, entered the home. He looked at the lifeless little body of the girl and said, "It's okay; she's only asleep." This stirred a response of nervous laughter from some curious onlookers gathered at the home. Undeterred by their ignorance, Jesus asked them to leave and moved toward the little girl. Then, in a deep calm, He took the little girl's hand and said, "Little girl, it's time to get up." At once she awoke and sat up. Jairus and the others were astonished and amazed. She was alive. It was never too late. Though it seemed that God was too slow, He really had never stopped moving toward the only daughter of Jairus. The delay was only in the mind of those living in the dimension of time. They were all witnesses of the heart of God, and fear was replaced with faith.

Settling the Issue of Fear

Jesus has a two-part solution to the problem of our fear. If we are to settle the issue of fear, we must follow the same instructions He gave to Jairus.

"Be Not Afraid..."

Jesus said to Jairus, *"Be not afraid...."* That may be more easily said than done when we are in the middle of a problem. You see, the greatest fear we have is that God does not care about us. We're afraid He won't hear us or pay attention to our needs. And the source of that fear is our not knowing the heart of God.

When God does not answer our prayers when and how we believe He should, we feel that He has turned

His back on us just as Jesus' back was turned toward Jairus when He stopped for the woman who had the issue of blood. In reality, Jesus had not turned His back on Jairus' need; He had merely stopped to acknowledge another need along the way. Jesus never stopped moving toward healing the daughter of Jairus.

From its first mention in the Bible, fear has been the result of thinking about God in limited human terms. Adam and his wife sinned against God and then hid themselves behind some bushes in fear. They heard the sound of God and reasoned that He was coming to punish them. But God's first words to them after they sinned were not words of revenge and anger. They were words of calling and invitation. God said, "Adam, where are you?" God was much more concerned about where Adam was than what he had done. He already knew what Adam had done; after all, God is God! When Adam heard God's footsteps, though, he was afraid, because he did not know the heart of God. And that is why you and I are sometimes afraid.

Again, the thing we fear most is that God does not care about us. When we believe the lie that God does not care, we also can come to believe that people don't care either. We fear that those family and friends whom we counted on might desert us in our time of greatest need. We are afraid that we are forgotten and forsaken.

When the twelve disciples were caught in a storm at sea, they became afraid. They did not fully know who Jesus was, and they accused Him of not caring about them. They did not realize that He was Jehovah Shalom Himself;

they did not understand that Peace was already there with them in the person of Jesus. (See Ephesians 2:14.)

> *And there arose a great storm of wind, and the waves beat into the ship, so that it was now full. And he was in the hinder part of the ship, asleep on a pillow: and they awake him, and say unto him, Master, carest thou not that we perish? And he arose, and rebuked the wind, and said unto the sea, Peace, be still. And the wind ceased, and there was a great calm. And he said unto them, Why are ye so fearful? how is it that ye have no faith? And they feared exceedingly, and said one to another, What manner of man is this, that even the wind and the sea obey him?* (Mark 4:37–41)

Jesus asked them, "Why are you afraid? Don't you trust Me?" They were all amazed, asking, *"What manner of man is this...?"* Their fear was based on the mistaken idea that somehow Jesus was not concerned about the storm they were in. And that is the same reason you and I sometimes become afraid. We feel, when we are caught in some storm or circumstance, that God does not care. Nothing could be further from the truth. Psalm 107 tells us that God sometimes moves us to *"do business in great waters"* (v. 23). How else would God build our faith but to draw us into waters that are over our heads? It is God who *"commandeth, and raiseth the stormy wind, which lifteth up the waves"* to bring us to our *"wit's end"* and to trust only Him (vv. 25, 27). We cannot learn to swim in the pool of faith if we stay in the shallow end, keeping our feet on the floor of the pool.

Jesus, who is our peace, is in the boat with us. He knows about the healing we need or the direction we

lack. He created that storm-tossed sea, and it is subject to His word alone. Remember, it was Jesus' idea to get into the boat in the first place! He knows where we are and where He is taking us. There is no reason to fear.

Jairus was in fear because of what he saw to be a delay in God's plan. Do you know anyone who can delay God? Think about it. Are you familiar with any force of nature that could stand in God's way if He was determined to act? God was not concerned when Israel stood on the shore of the Red Sea; He just moved it out of the way. God was not intimidated when Goliath taunted the army of Israel. He just appointed a little boy to knock him down with a stone. Nothing can stand in the way of God. As Paul said, nothing can separate us from the love of Christ. (See Romans 8:39.) At first the God whom Jairus knew was a limited God who was too late and too busy to love him and heal his daughter. But in the end he came to know a loving Savior who was never delayed in His concern for Jairus and his daughter. God is never too late. God is never too busy with something more important. However, we are not the ones to set God's agenda; He is. He may choose to move in an order and sequence that differs from ours. But we have no need to fear, for He has a purpose and an order even in our times of perceived delay.

"...Only Believe"

The second part of Jesus' instruction to settle Jairus' fear was *"...only believe."* The remedy for fear is faith. Faith and fear cannot reside in the same house. Belief and doubt cannot share the same address. Peace and anxiety cannot live together under the same roof. But what

exactly is faith? Faith is believing God; it is taking Him at His word. Keep in mind that our faith is not *for* a specific outcome; it is *in* God. As the psalmist said, *"Let all those that put their trust in thee rejoice: let them ever shout for joy, because thou defendest them: let them also that love thy name be joyful in thee"* (Psalm 5:11, emphasis added), and again, *"He shall not be afraid of evil tidings: his heart is fixed, trusting in the LORD"* (Psalm 112:7, emphasis added).

Fear is the result of unbelief. The only thing that can displace fear is our believing or trusting *in* God. The biblical word for trust is *faith.* But there is more than one kind of faith. Jana Bush, an avid student of the New Testament at my local church, shared with me an awesome teaching of James in James 2:14–26 that I want to present here. In these verses James described three kinds of faith. They are *dead* faith, *demonic* faith, and *dynamic* faith.

Dead faith is faith that is only intellectual. It is a mere mental opinion that is never evidenced outside our heads. For example, we may know in our minds the doctrine of salvation, but never really submit ourselves to God and trust Jesus for salvation. Thus our lives never change. James asked us,

> *What doth it profit, my brethren, though a man say he hath faith, and have not works? can faith save him?...Even so faith, if it hath not works, is dead, being alone.* (James 2:14, 17)

Dead faith mouths the right words but fails to back up those words with action. We say we believe, but we don't

live like we believe. This faith is dead because it gives us no power to live differently. We must go beyond mere mental opinion and live what we believe.

Then there is demonic faith. James said that *"the devils also believe, and tremble"* (James 2:19). The one with dead faith believes but does not live like he or she does. The one with demonic faith feels but does not obey. Instead, he or she is caught up in the emotion of things but never seems to grow past the feeling level. Yes, it is possible to feel something on an emotional level but never enter into trust and obedience. Demonic or "feeling" faith is an infatuation with God; it never goes beyond the surface to true love and trust. Can this kind of faith save? Again, no! A person can be enlightened in his or her mind and even stirred in his or her heart and still be lost! True saving faith involves something more, something that can be seen and recognized—a changed life! (See James 2:18.) Being a Christian involves trusting Christ and living for Christ! First you receive the life; then you reveal the life! This is what we term dynamic faith.

Dynamic faith is faith *in* God. The word *dynamic* implies change. Dynamic faith is a faith that flows with circumstances. It flows to fill in the gaps of perceived delays and a limited understanding of God and His ways. It is a faith that is proved by action. Our lives testify to what we really believe. Dynamic faith is based on knowing the heart of God, not on predicting how He might respond to our need. It is important to know that God is with us when we are in trouble, just as Jesus was in the boat with His disciples. He has said, *"He shall*

call upon me, and I will answer him: I will be with him in trouble; I will deliver him, and honour him" (Psalm 91:15). Knowing that God is with us in trouble allows us to have a dynamic faith that flows with circumstances. This faith allows us to weather those seasons of perceived delay because we know and trust the heart of God.

When we have dynamic faith, fear is replaced with faith, and unbelief with belief. It is in this faith that we are embraced until we are healed.

Healed

While sitting in the quiet of my own home two days after my cancer was diagnosed and the need for surgery indicated, I sensed the Lord saying that it would be all right for me to have the surgery. Somehow, as frightened as I was, I knew my Lord would restore me through this medical procedure. So I reached out to Jesus, just as the woman with the issue of blood did, trusting that He would work through the surgeon to heal me. At that moment, the Lord filled me with His peace, and I scheduled the surgery.

The seventy-two hours following my surgery were a blur of pain, anxiety, fear, and more fear as we awaited the final prognosis. Had they gotten all of the cancer? Would I need other treatments? Would I live or die? As I awoke on the third day after my surgery, a conversation taking place between my husband and physician began to penetrate my mind.

"Sir, we are happy to tell you that we got it all. Your wife is so fortunate. It's only a matter of time and healing. She will be just fine."

When I received the good medical report that changed my life, it was a message of faith, hope, and love from the heart of God. Though Jesus did not respond to my need for healing the way I might have expected, He did show up, and I was restored. He showed up in power and authority and healed my body according to His own plans and grace.

God may not always move in the way we expect. But, in reality, He never stops moving toward us. We also must realize that the enemy of our souls will do everything in his power to convince us that God does not care about us and that we are beyond God's ability to act. He will tell us that it's too late or that God is too busy for us. When these words of doubt and delay enter our hearts, all we need to do is remember that the current of God's compassion never stops flowing toward us. God is not delayed. As we invest our trust in the heart of God, as we walk in dynamic faith, He will speak words of peace to us, even in the midst of our fears.

Peace I leave with you, my peace I give unto you: not as the world giveth, give I unto you. Let not your heart be troubled, neither let it be afraid.
(John 14:27)

Personal Reflections

Chapter Six

"...I'm Broke"

Chapter Six

"...I'm Broke"

The Issue of Lack

This beginning of miracles did Jesus in Cana of Galilee, and manifested forth his glory; and his disciples believed on him.
—John 2:11

I t was so embarrassing. The invitations had been sent and all the details arranged for my daughter's wedding. The church, the reception, the limousines, the food—everything was set. The bridal gown and all the bridesmaid dresses were pressed and ready to be picked up, and the florist was calling to ask for the final payment. Everything from the wedding cake to the photographer was ready—that is, everything except my

bank account. We just didn't have enough resources to cover all the obligations. I thought to myself, *What will I tell my daughter? She's waited all her life for this wedding.*

Money wasn't the only thing that had run out. I was as exhausted as my bank account. I was running on empty. In a time when I should have been laughing and rejoicing, I was sinking deeper and deeper into a pit of debt and despair. Worry filled my mind and heart. *What if this just can't come together? What will our family and friends think?* My patience was wearing thin, and I just wanted to scream, "Stop! Enough already!" Here I was on the eve of this special day, and the only thought in my mind was "I'm broke!"

How many times have our well-laid plans blown up in our faces? How many times did the bills come in faster than the dollars to meet them? We think we have plenty, but then circumstances over which we have no control come along, and suddenly where we once had excess, now we have nothing. Where we once were in the "black," now we are in the "red." There is just "too much month left at the end of the money."

Two thousand years ago another potential wedding disaster loomed over a family in Cana of Galilee. There was another set of stressed-out parents trying to figure out what to do as whispers spread throughout the gathering that the wine was running low. This was a small town, a close community. The family was responsible for providing all the refreshments for a wedding feast that would go on for days. The bride and groom, along with

their families, would never live this down. The undercurrent of snickering grew stronger by the minute as friends and relatives began to surmise an apparent lack of preparation.

Put yourself in this family's position. What if you invited someone out to dinner, only to find that your credit card was over its limit? Think of the embarrassment. What would your guest think? What if it was your boss, or, heaven forbid, your in-laws? This was the dilemma these people faced in Cana.

A joyous marriage celebration had been going on for several days when Mary heard that the wine was running low. Knowing the social ramifications of this shortage, she went to the only One who could do anything about it: her son, Jesus. Mary said to Jesus, *"They have no wine"* (John 2:3).

What is it that is running low in your life? Where are you experiencing lack? Maybe there is a rumbling coming from your checking account like that from an empty stomach. Or perhaps the car has broken down or the dentist just told you that the kids need braces on their teeth. Regardless of our stature or station, we will encounter a shortfall or lack beyond our available resources at some time in our lives. The question is, what will we do with that issue of lack?

The Real Thing We Are Lacking

Sometimes it's not that we don't have what we need, but rather that our attitude about money and possessions needs to be adjusted. Even when we have money,

land, houses, cars, and "possessions," we can still yearn for something that money, possessions, and status can never satisfy—peace, loving-kindness, patience, and joy. Maybe what has run low is your time spent alone with God. I think that it is possible for us to be so caught up with and focused on our material needs that we forget about God.

Neil B. Wiseman states that too often too many of us have been seduced by the "good life" syndrome (*Growing Your Soul*, Grand Rapids, Michigan: Fleming H. Revell, 1992, p. 14). The "good life" describes our ferocious race to get "things" and the resulting loss of what really matters. Wiseman suggests that all of this is made even worse by the fact we have too little time, too many choices, too few values, too many demands, and too few abiding commitments. Our preoccupations with power, sex, busyness, and money have made the so-called good life lopsided. It's no wonder we feel "under-whelmed" by integrity, peace, and love.

Further, Wiseman shares that the good life, when represented by insatiable grasping, will wreck relationships, stress the heart, and sear the soul. As a result, the good life can easily turn into a hellish merry-go-round that never stops. Greed always wants more—a lot more—because greed fools us into behaving strangely. Scottish novelist and poet George MacDonald exposed this tricky snare of greed in one of his *Unspoken Sermons*. He said, "If it be things that slay you, what matters whether things you have, or things you have not?" (See www.ccel.org for MacDonald's *Unspoken Sermons 2*, under the chapter entitled "The Cause of Spiritual Stupidity.")

God has a purpose in our seasons of perceived lack. God, in His loving compassion, wants to wake us up and draw us to Himself so that He can fulfill what matters most—our soul and spirit. Whatever we have or do not have is incomplete without Christ. Jesus told us this plainly in Matthew 16:26: *"For what is a man profited, if he shall gain the whole world, and lose his own soul? or what shall a man give in exchange for his soul?"* Furthermore, a person who has everything but Christ will always be in need. Therefore, those who desire the authentic good life must make Jesus the center of their plans. Those who have everything but Christ have nothing. Those who have only Christ have everything.

It was neither an accident nor a coincidence that Jesus chose the wedding at Cana as His first recorded miracle. Marriage is a strong reminder of our relationship with God. Within the ancient understanding of marriage in Israel, it was implied that the husband was responsible to provide for the support of his wife. The husband provided all that the wife needed. Through this event, Jesus was pointing to the reality that the wine of our human production and effort will always run out. We cannot save ourselves, neither can we sustain ourselves. All that we need comes from the hand of our holy Bridegroom, Jesus. The old wine of human effort and expectation will always run out, but our needs can be met in the new wine of grace through Jesus Christ. From the moment we say "I do" to Jesus, He is the One who provides for us. It is not Jesus *plus* anything else. When we run out of our own wine, we must understand that Jesus is at the reception and that He is ready to transform our lack into His glory. But how is that new and miraculous wine of

grace released? It is released only when we turn to Jesus in faith, just as Mary did.

Settling the Issue of Lack

From the moment Mary turned to Jesus and said that the wine was running out, a new epoch was established. Jesus was no longer under His mother's authority; He was taking His place as Lord of all!

When Jesus was twelve years old, His family journeyed from Nazareth to Jerusalem for the feast of the Passover. It was on the homeward leg of the pilgrimage that His parents missed Him and turned back, only to find Him going *"about [His] Father's business"* (Luke 2:49). Mary *"kept all these sayings in her heart"* (v. 51), knowing the relationship that existed between Jesus and His heavenly Father. In time this relationship came to maturity as Jesus was baptized and initiated into His mission, as recorded in the Gospels. (See Matthew 3:13–17.) Jesus was the Son of His Father, and He was endued with the power of heaven to establish the kingdom of God on the earth. It was to the Son of God that Mary turned in faith when the lack presented itself—and we must do likewise.

Like a ship foundering at sea, Mary sent out a kind of "SOS" to Jesus to meet the crisis. She first had to *Seek* the Source, then *Obey* His instruction, and finally *See* His glory.

Seeking the Source

When Mary approached Jesus and said, *"They have no wine"* (John 2:3), she was seeking help from the

Source of all things. Indeed, Jesus' very mission on earth was to fill our need. There was no area of need that Jesus did not address in His ministry here on earth. When there was a need for healing, Jesus filled it. When there was a lack of food, Jesus turned a few loaves and fishes into a feast. Jesus is not an indifferent bystander in our times of need. No, He is the Creator and Sustainer of all that there is. He owns the *"cattle upon a thousand hills"* (Psalm 50:10). We tend to put our own human limitations and motivations on Jesus, but Jesus does not barter or bargain with us to meet our needs. He does not supply us because we have been good little girls and boys. He supplies our need because He can, and because He loves us!

> *For by him were all things created, that are in heaven, and that are in earth, visible and invisible, whether they be thrones, or dominions, or principalities, or powers: all things were created by him, and for him: and he is before all things, and by him all things consist.* (Colossians 1:16–17)

When we approach Jesus, we are laying our need at the feet of the One who is *"able to do exceeding abundantly above all that we ask or think, according to the power that worketh in us"* (Ephesians 3:20). God delights in our seeking Him. Don't we delight when our children come to us with a request that we can fulfill? How many times have we failed to seek the Source of all things, turning instead to the inadequate wine of human effort and reason? Perhaps our pride prevented us from approaching Him. Maybe we wanted to show our Father just how smart or talented we were. God is

not impressed when we try to do things without Him. God wants us to seek Him; He delights in our seeking Him. How would you feel if you were seated at a feast and one of your children sat starving outside your front door? Imagine how God feels when we do not seek Him for what we need.

At this point it might be good to differentiate between what we merely want and what we really need. If we recklessly spend and charge ourselves into a hole, we cannot expect God to pick up the tab. Imagine one of your children taking a credit card from your wallet to go on a spending spree. Would your child expect you to pay the bill when the credit card statement came in at the end of the month? In the same vein, would we go to the Lord tearfully begging for a vacation in Europe? God, who delights to give beyond our need, may give us that vacation simply because He loves us and wants to bless us. But we must clearly understand the difference between what we want and what we need.

When the wine ran out and Mary brought the need to Jesus, He responded by calling her *"woman"* and saying, *"What have I to do with thee? mine hour is not yet come"* (John 2:4). He would address her this way one more time when He hung from the cross. (See John 19:26.) This was not a tone of disrespect, but one of affection and honor. The Lord does not look down upon us or speak to us in exalted rhetoric when we seek Him; rather, He responds to our need in compassion. With His utterance, Mary began to relate to her son in a new way. She sought Him now not as her son, but as her Messiah. She approached Jesus in a submissive and patient humility, trusting in

His heart. She was not thinking of herself or worried about how she might look to those around her. She just quietly listened to His response, driven to see that the needs of the wedding were met—"more wine."

When we find ourselves in genuine need, we can seek the Source of all things, and He will supply our needs *"according to his riches in glory by Christ Jesus"* (Philippians 4:19). But it is not enough that we seek the Source; we also must be prepared for Him to respond in any way He sees fit. We must be ready to obey whatever the Lord instructs.

Obey His Instruction

God may not always meet our need the way we plan or imagine that He will. How many times have we prayed for God to move in a specific way, only to see Him do something completely unheard of? When Israel languished in bondage in Egypt for those many years, no one could have predicted that God would deliver them by the hand of an eighty-year-old fugitive shepherd languishing in the wilderness. And who would have expected the calling of God to come from a burning bush? Search the Bible, and you'll see that God used only one burning bush. God is not bound to meet our needs according to our understanding, but according to His riches in glory. God moves in ways unique to Him that result in bringing Him glory.

When Mary brought a need to Jesus, she prepared everyone for His response. *"His mother saith unto the servants, Whatsoever he saith unto you, do it"* (John

2:5). When we face the issue of lack, we, too, must be willing to do whatever Jesus tells us. There was no specific prescription, no preordained understanding as to how Jesus would respond to the need when the servants approached Him. There was only obedience.

Our obedience is not always a simple or single matter; rather, it will always require that we trust the heart of God. I had to trust in God's heart when, with tears running down my face, I slipped to my tired, worn knees and cried to the Lord for help. I needed the favor of God to keep my daughter's wedding from slipping from a dream into a nightmare. The natural wine of my own resources and ability had run out, and I sought the wine of God's grace. The grace of God cannot flow when we are trying to provide for our needs in our own strength. Self-effort becomes a bottleneck to the flow of God's grace. It's good when we are tired and have nowhere else to go but to Jesus Christ for help. For Jesus has the power to meet not only the material need, but also the needs of our hearts. I didn't doubt that the Lord would respond to my lack as I reached out to Him. But I could not have imagined how He would fill it.

At the wedding feast of Cana in Galilee, Jesus instructed the servants, *"Fill the waterpots with water"* (John 2:7). Now, to us the instruction appears to be very simple. However, history reports that these waterpots held 20 to 30 gallons apiece. If these waterpots were to be filled, it would require the efforts of several people. Often God will address our lack through the help of other people. If we are too proud to ask for help, we may miss a miracle. God did not design us to work alone. We

must be open with others about our need and perhaps risk embarrassment.

God can bring us instruction through others in the body or through His written Word. God can also instruct us by the hand of leaders to whom we are in submission. Whatever the means, we must be ready to obey His instructions to the full. We must fill the waterpots to the brim. We can leave no room for human methods. There can be no dilution of the wine of His grace. If we are to settle the issue of lack, then we must be ready to obey whatever the Lord tells us to do.

For me, it was a matter of finding Jesus in my personal prayer closet. There I let out my fears, my concerns, and my questions. Then I simply asked, "Jesus, what should I do?" The Lord spoke to me clearly as I lay at His feet.

See His Glory

Somewhere between filling the pots and bearing what was drawn out to the man in charge, Jesus did what the servants could not do for themselves. He performed a miracle. Isn't that what a miracle is? He transformed their issue of lack into an opportunity to put His power on display. And the wine He created was so excellent in vintage that the man in charge declared,

> Every man at the beginning doth set forth good wine; and when men have well drunk, then that which is worse: but thou hast kept the good wine until now. (John 2:10)

As a result, the glory of God was seen, and Jesus was believed. Is that not His purpose in our season of lack? When we turn to Jesus, He releases new wine to us. It is this new wine that reveals His glory. And when His glory is revealed, we and others grow in faith—we believe Him.

How important is the glory of God? The glory of God is the manifestation of who and what God is. The glory of the Lord is everything that makes God be God. It is all of His characteristics—His surpassing greatness. God manifests His glory—and all that He is—to us to reveal His heart to us, and to call us to Himself in greater dimensions of power and purpose.

God truly provided for my daughter's wedding in a way that only He could. As I was on my face before the Lord, the telephone rang. I thought, *Who is calling me? Don't they know I'm praying?* I answered the phone. The voice on the other end of the line calmly asked how I was doing. (It was obvious that I had been crying.) I opened my heart to this precious and caring sister and told her about my lack. She responded by telling me that the Lord had moved her to call me and that I was not to cancel anything. The Lord would provide. The word that was shared lodged within me. Instantly, the heaviness was replaced with the praise of God. I knew that somehow God would supply my need as I began to celebrate His presence and power.

Shortly thereafter, someone showed up at my door and handed me an envelope. When I opened it, I found thousands of dollars. A little while later a package arrived

at the door, and it, too, held thousands of dollars. Still another envelope of money addressed to my daughter and myself showed up at the office. None of the people used by the Lord to bless us had talked to one another. Meanwhile, I was gasping at the glory of God! The Lord had far exceeded my ability and expectation. In a matter of hours, mourning had turned into dancing, lack into celebration, and poverty into prosperity. He performed a miracle that resulted not only in a beautiful wedding for my daughter, but also in a greater revelation of the glory of God!

> *But my God shall supply all your need according to his riches in glory by Christ Jesus. Now unto God and our Father be glory for ever and ever. Amen.*
> (Philippians 4:19–20)

Personal Reflections

Chapter Seven

"...I'm Too Young"

Chapter Seven

"...I'm Too Young"

The Issue of Disqualification

Then said I, Ah, Lord GOD! behold, I cannot speak: for I
am a child.
—Jeremiah 1:6

"You're too young; this is adult business. Why don't you just go outside and play like the other kids?" I heard words like these many times as I was growing up. My parents encouraged me in playing the organ and the piano, but not when it came to other, more serious issues of ministry and the things of the Spirit.

Growing up, I enjoyed Sunday school classes and youth activities, but I was also excited about worship and

teaching and our times of celebration. Somehow, I always felt older than my peers. I had fun as a child and a teen, but the things that stood out to me were the times when I grew in discernment and the things of the Spirit. Even at a young age I was spiritually aware. I could walk into a room and immediately sense whether or not someone was ill, someone's heart was broken, or even if someone was hungry.

It was difficult for my parents to understand me. I didn't always understand myself! I knew I was just a kid, but sometimes I preferred to sit in an adult Bible study and learn about Jesus rather than pass notes and giggle in the back of the church. I preferred to attend prayer meetings with the older women rather than play with dolls. People said that *I was too young to be so old.*

Many times I was concerned about the grown-up matters of the ministry. I prayed for my father and mother as they administered the church. Sometimes the Lord would speak a word of warning or direction to me that I would share with them. Once the Lord spoke to me very clearly, warning me about a man whom my father was about to appoint to a ministry position. Though I passed on the warning, I was politely directed to stand aside and allow the adults to handle the church. As it ended up, my father had a difficult time with that man for many years. So many times I felt frustrated and set aside; nonetheless, the Lord continued to speak, and I continued to communicate what He spoke.

One time in my frustration I asked the Lord, "What good is it to know what I know (though I can't explain

how I know it)? What good is it to hear what I hear (though I can't explain how I hear it)? Why do I continue to see what I see if I cannot share it? Lord, am I too young? Am I just a kid?"

Many of us struggle with issues that sound something like this one. Many of us are told that we are too young, too old, not experienced enough (or maybe too experienced), or not educated sufficiently to serve God in some way. There are always those who are willing to disqualify us in some form or fashion. Perhaps it's to protect their own ministry turf, or maybe it's out of some other jealous motive. But the simple fact is that the burdens we feel and the gifts we evidence have little to do with our age or experience. The anointing of God is more powerful than the stifling of men.

So what are we to do? How should preteen prophets and adolescent apostles respond to the word of the Lord? Are they being disrespectful or rebellious if they speak? Is it just that they are untaught? And what of the senior saint in whom the word of the Lord reverberates as easily as the aged wood of a Stradivarius violin? Are we to discount or disregard fresh words of the new believer who hears the word of God in excited innocence? Are the elderly disqualified from use in the kingdom of God because of age or previous experience? If God can speak *to* vessels of various ages, then why can He not speak *through* them?

One day as I sat quietly reading my Bible, a passage from the prophet Jeremiah caught my eye. It seems that the prophet Jeremiah had a similar problem. Jeremiah thought that he was too young and too inexperienced to

deliver the word of God. Why would anyone listen to one who was so young? Wouldn't people just laugh at him? Who would take a child seriously? My eyes were drawn to these verses.

> *Then the word of the LORD came unto me, saying, Before I formed thee in the belly I knew thee; and before thou camest forth out of the womb I sanctified thee, and I ordained thee a prophet unto the nations. Then said I, Ah, Lord GOD! behold, I cannot speak: for I am a child. But the LORD said unto me, Say not, I am a child: for thou shalt go to all that I shall send thee, and whatsoever I command thee thou shalt speak. Be not afraid of their faces: for I am with thee to deliver thee, saith the LORD. Then the LORD put forth his hand, and touched my mouth. And the LORD said unto me, Behold, I have put my words in thy mouth.*
> (Jeremiah 1:4–9)

Reading a little closer, these words seemed to leap off the pages: "I *knew* you…I *sanctified* you…I *ordained* you…." This is God's response to the words of disqualification that we sometimes hear—that we are too young, too old, too new, or too something to be used by God. God is not a *"respecter of persons"* or human understanding (Acts 10:34). That which burns in our hearts, unquenched by human reason, is the Word of God, and it will not be silenced.

Settling the Issue of Disqualification

The way to settle the issue of disqualification is to understand God's qualifications for service in His kingdom. It's very simple, really. Those who are called to

serve God are those whom God *knows, sanctifies,* and *ordains* for His purpose and calling.

"I Knew You..."

If we are used by God in ministry, it is because of the relationship that exists between God and ourselves. God uses us because He knows us.

Jeremiah responded to the call of God like many of us do. Even after he was assured that God was calling him, he still offered reasons and excuses why he could not respond to the call. Isn't that just human nature? God, the Creator of the universe, puts us in position to do great things, and immediately we tell Him that He must have the wrong person. We offer Him all kinds of reasons why He must have mistaken us for someone more worthy or qualified. "I'm too young" is only one of the reasons we offer. We may say, "But God, I'm a sinner," or "God, I had an abortion," or "God, I've only just gotten saved," or "God, I don't have a seminary degree." The list goes on and on, but even before He calls us, God knows all the details of our lives that we give as excuses.

God saw us in our struggles. God saw us in that life-style we used to live. Perhaps that is why He called us in the first place. Who better to minister to a drug addict than a former drug addict? Who could better evangelize children than a child? Who could be a more effective marriage counselor than one whose marriage had been broken but then restored by the grace of God? Paul told us that we can *"comfort them which are in any trouble, by the comfort wherewith we ourselves are comforted of*

God" (2 Corinthians 1:4). God does not call us *despite* our issues, but perhaps *because* of them.

God calls us and uses us because He knows us, yes, but He also calls us because we know Him. The most important ministry we have is to God Himself. Jesus knew that His first ministry was to be in union with the Father. How many times did Jesus go to be alone with the Father before entering a new realm of ministry? Jesus said,

> *The Son can do nothing of himself, but what he seeth the Father do: for what things soever he doeth, these also doeth the Son likewise. For the Father loveth the Son, and showeth him all things that himself doeth: and he will show him greater works than these, that ye may marvel.* (John 5:19–20)

Ministry done outside of our intimate connection to Christ is in done in the flesh, not out of love for God. Again, Jesus said,

> *Many will say to me in that day, Lord, Lord, have we not prophesied in thy name? and in thy name have cast out devils? and in thy name done many wonderful works? And then will I profess unto them, I never knew you: depart from me, ye that work iniquity.* (Matthew 7:22–23)

How many in the church today minister out of their desire for recognition rather than their love for Christ? The most vital and fulfilling ministry any of us has is our ministry to the person of Jesus Christ in our worship and devotion to Him. If we don't get that right, then nothing else matters.

"I Sanctified You..."

Because God knows us, He also sets us apart, or sanctifies us. To be sanctified means that we are set apart as God's special property. Just like a favorite pen that we use to write only love letters, God sets us apart with a unique combination of spiritual abilities and experience to be effective in His kingdom. Jeremiah was set apart by God to fulfill the role of prophet to the nations. His prophetic gift was not one that brought him fame. Instead, for the most part it brought him misery.

Jeremiah did not attend prophetic conferences, neither did he enjoy any great privilege in the religious community. On the contrary, his high position got him thrown to the bottom of a muddy well. But somehow God knew the man whom He had set apart for this ministry. Though Jeremiah did not understand what God was doing and complained bitterly, the fire in his bones to preach the word of God was never dampened. (See Jeremiah 20:9.) God knows us well. He knows what He is doing and how we fit into His plans. When we discern the calling of God on our lives, we can be assured that God will not throw us into water over our heads and let us drown. Many times in my own ministry I was not sure that I would survive the challenges that came my way. But God knew whom He had called, and He knew where that calling would carry me, and so gave me the grace to see it through. God is so good!

"I Ordained You..."

God knows us and has set us apart for His purpose, but we do not fulfill that purpose in our own power and

ability. God also *ordains* us. To be ordained is to be given the authority and power to fulfill the calling of God.

Think for a minute about a traffic jam where several cars are moving around in confusion with angry people blowing their horns. Then, one small man sees the motorized mess and decides on his own to do something about it. So he gets out of his own car and runs into the traffic, waving his arms and trying to bring it into order. He is only one person, though, and he is soon overwhelmed by the traffic. But if you took that same man and put a police uniform on him and a badge on his chest, the cars would have to obey him and move in order. What makes the difference? The police officer is successful because the badge represents authority. He has been sent with the power and authority to do the job. And spiritually, so have you!

We cannot minister just where we please and then expect God to bless our ministry. No, God *sends* us; He authorizes us to act on His behalf. And when He ordained Jeremiah, He told the young prophet not to worry or be afraid of those who might question or intimidate him.

> But the LORD said unto me, Say not, I am a child: for thou shalt go to all that I shall send thee, and whatsoever I command thee thou shalt speak. Be not afraid of their faces: for I am with thee to deliver thee, saith the LORD. Then the LORD put forth his hand, and touched my mouth. And the LORD said unto me, Behold, I have put my words in thy mouth. (Jeremiah 1:7–9)

There is no limitation or disqualification for those who minister under the hand of God. God knows us, sets us apart, and then sends us out. It is God who sends us. It is God's word that we speak. It is God's hand that is upon our ministry and us. *"Say not, I am a child."*

God Will Qualify You

The apostle Paul comforted a young minister by telling him, *"Let no man despise thy youth; but be thou an example of the believers, in word, in conversation, in charity, in spirit, in faith, in purity"* (1 Timothy 4:12). Don't let anyone disqualify you because you are too young, too old, inexperienced, undereducated, a woman, a new convert, a struggling saint, or any other label. The most important qualification for ministry is simply responding to the call of God. When we respond, the God who knows you, sanctifies you, and ordains you will also qualify you to serve Him for His own purpose and glory.

Personal Reflections

Chapter Eight

"...I'm Sinking"

Chapter Eight

"...I'm Sinking"

The Issue of Failure

And straightway Jesus constrained his disciples to get into a
ship, and to go before him unto the other side, while he sent
the multitudes away. And when he had sent the multitudes
away, he went up into a mountain apart to pray: and when
the evening was come, he was there alone. But the ship was
now in the midst of the sea, tossed with waves: for the wind
was contrary. And in the fourth watch of the night Jesus went
unto them, walking on the sea. And when the disciples saw
him walking on the sea, they were troubled, saying, It is a
spirit; and they cried out for fear. But straightway Jesus spake
unto them, saying, Be of good cheer; it is I; be not afraid. And
Peter answered him and said, Lord, if it be thou, bid me come
unto thee on the water. And he said, Come. And when Peter

was come down out of the ship, he walked on the water, to
go to Jesus. But when he saw the wind boisterous, he was
afraid; and beginning to sink, he cried, saying, Lord, save me.
And immediately Jesus stretched forth his hand, and caught
him, and said unto him, O thou of little faith, wherefore didst
thou doubt? And when they were come into the ship, the wind
ceased. Then they that were in the ship came and worshipped
him, saying, Of a truth thou art the Son of God.
—Matthew 14:22-33

*D*on't you just love Peter? He was always the first and the loudest one to respond to the challenges that came along. It was Peter who dropped his tattered nets at the invitation of Jesus to follow. It was Peter who was in the inner circle of the Master and who witnessed all the great things that Jesus did in those three dynamic years of ministry. It was Peter who was the first to dare to recognize Jesus as the Messiah. It was Peter who witnessed *life restored* to the daughter of Jairus. It was Peter who witnessed true *life revealed* as the glory of God encompassed Jesus on the Mount of Transfiguration. And it was Peter who witnessed *life surrendered* in the garden as Jesus sweat drops of blood in prayer. Peter was a guy who was on the cutting edge of what God was doing.

Peter was a man who simply trusted Jesus and was determined to follow Him wherever He led. He didn't always know where he was going, but he was determined to get there before anyone else! You could say that Peter's mode of life was "ready, fire, aim!" He was ready to die for Jesus before he knew what it meant to live for Him. At least when Peter did mess up, he did so at full speed.

Perhaps the greatest thing we can say about Peter is that he responded to the unknown and the unheard of by simply believing and stepping out in faith toward whatever Jesus said or did. He just trusted Jesus. So it is no great surprise that Peter was the one to jump out of the boat and begin to walk on water with Jesus. It just fits him.

Then it happened—Peter, this man of great faith who enjoyed a close and intimate relationship with Jesus, began to sink beneath the waves. You and I also experience times of sinking. Like Peter, we have enjoyed personal intimacy with the Lord. Like Peter, we have witnessed the power and the glory of God displayed in the earth. And like Peter, we have stepped out of the boat and begun to walk toward Jesus, only to find ourselves sinking beneath the waves as we waver in our faith.

There was a time when I decided to take greater personal responsibility for my health, which led me to change my eating habits. After a couple of months I had lost seventeen pounds and felt great. I was so excited about my new life. I thanked the Lord for changing my life through understanding the truth of His Word about my overeating. The Lord had called forth a new woman who was healthier and happier. Without hesitation, I gave God the glory.

Fast-forward two months. The wardrobe of this new woman was becoming a little tight. In reality, there was nothing wrong with the clothing. My wardrobe had not decreased; I had increased! That "new woman" went back looking for her old ways and found a willing traveling partner: *Mrs. Callendar.* We met at Mrs. Callendar's Pie

House with increasing regularity. At first it was once a week for a slice of her fresh peach strawberry or peach pie. Then it became a once-a-day habit. *God, help me. I'm sinking again.*

I had been doing so well and was so proud of the new woman I had become that I forgot to talk to God about her. At first I prayed each morning and asked for guidance and strength to maintain wise eating habits. But as time went by, I would go days without prayer about it. I had taken my eyes off the One who led me to my new condition, and I began to sink.

Despite our best efforts and obedience, all of us will sink into failure at some time in our Christian lives. The scope of our failures can range from eating too much pie to not extending grace to someone who sins against us. Regardless of how it happens, there are times when we find ourselves sinking beneath the waves of failure and disappointment. And each time we sink, our feelings of guilt become greater. We find ourselves asking, "How could this happen to me? How can someone who loves the Lord so much fail so miserably?" But thank God, our failures do not spell the end of our relationship with God or our ministry. Rather, they become opportunities for growth in the grace and knowledge of Jesus Christ. (See 2 Peter 3:18.)

We Must Try before We Can Fail

And straightway Jesus constrained his disciples to get into a ship, and to go before him unto the other side, while he sent the multitudes away.

(Matthew 14:22)

The first thing we must realize about failure is that we cannot fail when we do not try. You see, great failures and great faith are linked together.

Have you ever watched a baby take his or her first step? Before babies try to walk, they crawl along the floor, and perhaps pull themselves up and around on the furniture. But somehow, in their little baby minds, they decide that crawling is just not going to get them where they want to go. After watching the big people walking around them for a while, they decide to get up and walk. So with the aid of Mommy or Daddy, or perhaps with the help of a piece of furniture, they pull themselves up onto their chubby little legs. Then, with great delight, they take that first giggling step—and promptly fall straight back down, usually onto that part of them where God has provided suitable padding to cushion the fall. So then what? Do they just sit there and decide that crawling is good enough for them? Do they give up on walking after the first or the second or the fifteenth fall? No! They learn something each time, and with each attempt their little legs gain strength and experience. Eventually, after numerous falls, they begin to walk. Yes, they will still fall occasionally—and so will we—but they are walking nonetheless. The point is that they could not fail if they did not try in the first place.

Failures often begin as great steps of faith. In the incident when Peter sank, it was Jesus who got everybody in the boat and pushed them off in the direction of the other shoreline. It's not hard to get into the boat. Maybe we heard a great teaching or we saw a wonder of God, and we jumped into the boat. At first the direction seemed

to be clear and the destination attainable. Perhaps we launched ourselves out into some new area of ministry, or maybe we sensed the Lord calling us to some kind of mission field. So we set out in our little sailboat toward the other side, watching our sail filling with the wind and thinking about how wonderful things will be on that other shore. We envision ourselves being carried along by the prevailing wind of God's Spirit. After all, He has called us, and He will get us there, right? Everything is as it should be.

> *But the ship was now in the midst of the sea, tossed with waves: for the wind was contrary.*
> (Matthew 14:24)

Now, after we are away from the familiar shoreline, something strange seems to be happening. When we started, the winds seemed to carry us right out into the center of God's heart and calling. We were moving along and could almost smell the shoreline of our destination. But now, far away from home, the wind and the waves seem to be opposing us. We struggle to figure out which way the wind is blowing so we can get our sails into it, but there is no clear direction. The wind and waves of dark and unfamiliar seas beat against us and oppose us. We can no longer see either shoreline. We are in deep trouble.

"God, where are You? You told me to get into the boat. This was Your idea, God! What are You doing to me?" Don't we usually ask those kinds of questions when we experience failure or resistance? We assume, when we have answered the call of God and are in the will of God,

that we will be carried along by the wind of the Spirit. When we have said yes to God, the last thing we expect to do is fail. But it may be that God needed to get us out into deep waters so that He could speak to us. You see, it is the deepest waters that require the deepest trust. As long as we are standing on familiar shores, we think we know what God wants and where He is leading us. But when we respond to the invitation of God, He will bring us to the place where only He can find us—and where only He can save us.

This sea upon which we are sailing is life in the real world. It is the place where wind and waves beat against us as we pursue greater dimensions of Christ and ministry. It is a sea whose currents don't always seem to carry us toward the calling of God. There are contrary winds that resist our spiritual progress. Among these unwelcome winds is the wind of carnality, which wages war against the things of the Spirit, diverting us from the glory of God to the glory of personal recognition. Then there is the wind of disappointment; it is felt each time someone wounds us or doesn't live up to his or her identity in Christ. There is the wind of lust that seduces us into false intimacy and away from our deepening relationship with God. These and many other winds blow against us, flooding our boats and slowing our progress.

In the midst of this sea, when nothing seems to be as it should be, the Lord Himself comes walking in victory across the waves of uncertainty. He reveals His true identity in the deepest waters and invites us to *"come"* to Him. (See Matthew 14:29.)

Peter responded immediately to Jesus' invitation. He was willing to leave behind the boat of the familiar, the last vestige of safety. If the Lord is really going to lay hold of us and reveal Himself to us, it will not be in the boat of the familiar and the comfortable. It will be as we step out of the boat in total trust.

Ultimately our faith is not in what the Lord might do for us, but in the person of Jesus. Peter said, in effect, "If it is really You, Lord, I will be able to come to You." (See Matthew 14:28.) Peter believed in what the Lord could do, or maybe he believed in what he could do in the Lord. But when the winds of opposition and complications became *"boisterous"* (v. 30), Peter listened to them instead and took his eyes off Jesus. Peter forgot that it was Jesus who got him out of the boat to take those first steps. (And we forget that Peter actually walked on water!) Our failures are the result of forgetting that our faith is the result of a personal relationship. Circumstances may change and winds kick up, but the Lord, the One whom we trust it, does not change.

> *Ye are of God, little children, and have overcome them: because greater is he that is in you, than he that is in the world.* (1 John 4:4)

Settling the Issue of Failure

We must settle a few things about the issue of failure. Two of those things are, how does God respond to our failure, and how should we?

If we are to settle the issue of failure, then we must do so in the context of our personal and intimate relationship

with Jesus Christ. When Peter began to slip beneath the waves, it was to the person of Jesus that he cried out, *"Lord, save me"* (Matthew 14:30). Peter did not turn to one of the others in the boat. He did not ask for a life preserver or for some swimming tips. Peter called out to Jesus, the One whom Peter knew, the One who got Peter in the boat and then out of it. If we are to deal with failure, then it will be by trusting in Jesus.

> *Who is he that overcometh the world, but he that believeth that Jesus is the Son of God?* (1 John 5:5)

Notice Jesus' response to the sinking failure of Peter. ***"Immediately** Jesus stretched forth his hand, and caught him"* (Matthew 14:31, emphasis added). How long did Jesus wait to catch Peter? Jesus didn't take the time to discuss with Peter the principles he needed to remember about walking on water. Nor did Jesus say, "Hey, Peter, you're failing again. You'll never amount to anything." Jesus didn't allow Peter to begin to drown so that he could think about what he had done. No! Jesus stretched out His hand *"immediately"*! The instant that grace was needed, it was there. The only requirement was that Peter needed to know that he could not save himself, that only Jesus was in a position to do so. We think grace is applied to us only in our initial salvation experience. But Peter was already in an intimate relationship with Jesus. God's grace continues to save us each time we start to sink.

Jesus diagnosed Peter's problem. He said, *"O thou of little faith, wherefore didst thou doubt?"* (v. 31). He told Peter that the problem was that his faith was circumstantial. In other words, his faith lasted only until the wind

came up. Jesus told us that in the world we would have trouble; we would lose our focus and sink into circumstances. But the greater promise is that He has *"overcome the world"* (John 16:33). Christ has overcome the wind and the waves that try to swamp us. Whether we stand or fall, Jesus is the anchor that holds us steady until the winds stop.

Many times we waver in our faith. Our faith seems to last only long enough for problems to come along. It's like our one foot is rooted in our trust in God, but our other foot is on a banana peel that slips around on some temporary circumstance. Paul told us that this

> *light affliction, which is but for a moment, worketh for us a far more exceeding and eternal weight of glory; while we look not at the things which are seen, but at the things which are not seen: for the things which are seen are temporal; but the things which are not seen are eternal.*
>
> (2 Corinthians 4:17–18)

We tend to look at the problem instead of the Lord. And when we fail in some way, we continue to look at the failure in guilt. Guilt leads to shame, and shame leads to separation from God. But all of these are unnecessary! Christ is there to catch hold of our hand. However, we must overcome pride and allow Him to pull us out of our sinking condition.

Finally, we need to know what Jesus thinks about us in our occasional seasons of sinking. Does God hold a grudge against us when we fail? Where does God go when we backslide or lose focus? The answer is that God does

not hold a grudge, neither will He go anywhere. When Jesus pulled Peter up out of the raging sea, He did not just walk away from him. Jesus got right back into the same boat with Peter. There was no interruption of their intimate relationship; there was only love and peace. The wind had *"ceased"* (Matthew 14:32). The result was that Peter's personal knowledge and relationship with Jesus grew all the more. *"Then they that were in the ship came and worshipped him, saying, Of a truth thou art the Son of God"* (v. 33). What else would we do when we fall and Jesus picks us up again, but worship Him? When I tripped over the pie wagon and fell, it was God who called me back to Himself. The Lord restored that "new woman," but now this new woman would remember forever who had made her new. What else can I do but praise Him?

There will be times when you and I will sink and lapse into failure. But in those times the Lord will climb back into that boat with us and lead us to the next great thing that He is doing.

> *The LORD is gracious, and full of compassion; slow to anger, and of great mercy. The LORD is good to all: and his tender mercies are over all his works. All thy works shall praise thee, O LORD; and thy saints shall bless thee. They shall speak of the glory of thy kingdom, and talk of thy power; to make known to the sons of men his mighty acts, and the glorious majesty of his kingdom. Thy kingdom is an everlasting kingdom, and thy dominion endureth throughout all generations. **The LORD upholdeth all that fall, and raiseth up all those that be bowed down.***
> (Psalm 145:8–14, emphasis added)

Personal Reflections

Chapter Nine

***

"...I'm Wounded"

"...I'm Wounded"

The Issue of Past Hurts

And Jonathan, Saul's son, had a son that was lame of his feet. He was five years old when the tidings came of Saul and Jonathan out of Jezreel, and his nurse took him up, and fled: and it came to pass, as she made haste to flee, that he fell, and became lame. And his name was Mephibosheth.
—2 Samuel 4:4

She was a bright little girl—the light of her parents' lives. Her face seemed to glow with promise and possibility. Even at an early age she was being prepared for something special in the kingdom of God, and those around her could sense it. The warm safety of her surroundings made her a trusting child who loved and

enjoyed a life without fear in the bosom of her family and friends. All was as it should have been, until the day and the moment when a trusted family friend and minister touched her in a way that no friend, no shepherd would. He attempted to steal her innocence to feed his own perverted lust for pleasure and power. In a moment's time, he shattered her peace and left her numbed and confused.

She didn't know what to do or how to tell anyone what had happened. She had been abused and violated by one whom they all knew as a friend, someone whom everybody trusted. And though she was only a child and had done nothing wrong, she felt guilty and ashamed. She attempted to tell her mother what happened, but her mother chose to deny what she had been told. The young girl felt twice betrayed as the sin of this man was swept quietly under the rug. So the child was stripped of her esteem, her joy, her trust, and her belief that she was beautifully created in the image of God. She would find it difficult ever to trust anyone again, including the Lord. She felt dirty and defective. A bright little girl disappeared with that ungodly touching, and an abused child took her place, one who walked with a decided limp.

As the years passed, the wounded little girl became a lamed adult. On the outside she is the picture of maturity and success, yet inside she is still that abused little girl struggling to believe what God has said of her. It has been many years since the time of abuse, but part of her has been frozen in time since that moment of unthinkable violation. And though she has been counseled, prayed

with, and comforted, every now and then this "past issue" spawns new issues in her life. There are times when she is filled with the same terror and shame she felt at that time of lost innocence. She still finds it difficult to invest her trust in anyone. Even those God-ordained times of intimacy with her husband are bound to that intrusive instant of shattered trust.

This woman has grown weary of hiding her issue of woundedness. As a result, she reaches out to other damaged "little girls and boys," telling them that God loves them and that He will set them free—but she has trouble believing it herself. And so she limps through life, chained to a moment in time, waiting to be released to run again.

Walking Wounded

The account of this little girl is true and all too common both inside and outside the body of Christ. There are so many other little boys and girls who have been wounded in one way or another. They gather together for fellowship as if at a masquerade ball, hidden behind religious masks of wholeness. But behind the masks resides such great pain that it causes them to limp through a life in which terror and shame lie in wait for the next reminder of those earlier wounds. These people are not what they appear to be. Many victims of abuse live with fear and a sense of shame, even though what happened to them was not their fault. Living with this false guilt then leads them to spend their whole lives proving their worth to the world. They live with a limp, and they frequently end up in relationships that lead to even more abuse.

None of this is God's design. God did not choose for some to walk through life halted and lamed with disfiguring wounds from the past. God does not desire for us to live in separation and limitation. Somehow the abused ones convince themselves that this is God's plan for their lives, that they must just learn to live with it. But what purpose, what glory could there be to God for one person to live under the power and influence of past wounds? The truth is that the Lord desires for all who touch Him to be healed. God calls Himself *Yaveh Rhapha,* "the Lord our Healer." (See Exodus 15:26.) He is the One who puts us back together when we are wounded.

The Bible tells us of another who was wounded as a child while in the hands of a trusted servant. His name was Mephibosheth, the son of Jonathan and a prince of Israel.

Settling the Issue of Past Wounds

The kingdom of Israel was in a tumult. The kingdom and the house of Saul had been shaken to their very foundations. Saul, the first king of Israel, was dead by his own hand. Jonathan, the son of Saul and covenant friend of David, had been killed in a losing battle. All those who remained in the house of Saul ran for their lives to escape any reprisal from the new king—David. In her frenzied panic, the nurse who cared for Mephibosheth, the son of Jonathan, dropped him, and he became lame in both legs. (See 2 Samuel 4:4.)

After the kingdom was whole and at rest, David, the great king of Israel, asked whether there was anyone left

from the house of Saul to whom he might show kindness. It was revealed that there was yet alive a son of his covenant friend Jonathan. (See 2 Samuel 9:1, 3.) This son was living more or less in hiding at the house of Machir in a place called Lodebar. Lodebar (which means "pastureless") was a place of desolation and separation from the world. It is the place where all those who are abused find themselves—cut off from the world by their own shame.

Mephibosheth lived in a place of self-banishment under the weight of the generational sin begun by his grandfather, Saul. Saul had disobeyed God and pursued his own glory. The result was a blanket of shame and infamy over his house. In this shame his grandson, Mephibosheth, had no name and no holdings. In addition to generational sin, Mephibosheth also suffered the lameness of his wounding as a small child. As one who was lame, he would be cut off from any religious celebration and have no social standing. He was forced to live off the charity of others, without hope our future.

Mephibosheth is a picture of the walking wounded in the world today—those who live sad lives of limitation because of previous wounding. They live in separation, limping through life far below their birthright. Think about it—Mephibosheth was born to royalty, a prince of Israel. But through no fault of his own, he was wounded and unable to walk in the power and destiny that should have been his. His surroundings at Lodebar and the twisted condition of his own feet were constant reminders of his lot. He lived a nameless, powerless, and hopeless existence. That is, he did until the day that the great

king called for one over whom his covenant grace could flow.

Healing the Wounds

When Mephibosheth was taken to the king, his wounds were quite obvious.

> *Now when Mephibosheth, the son of Jonathan, the son of Saul, was come unto David, he fell on his face, and did reverence. And David said, Mephibosheth. And he answered, Behold thy servant! And David said unto him, Fear not: for I will surely show thee kindness for Jonathan thy father's sake, and will restore thee all the land of Saul thy father; and thou shalt eat bread at my table continually. And he bowed himself, and said, What is thy servant, that thou shouldest look upon such a dead dog as I am?* (2 Samuel 9:6–8)

Mephibosheth referred to himself as a *"dead dog."* What could be lower than a dead dog? He, like all who suffer wounds, held himself in low regard. He was probably shocked that the king hadn't sent for him to kill him and thus destroy the last remnant of Saul's house. Mephibosheth saw himself as worthless before the king. He was unable to move beyond his past wounding. But the king knew of his condition and still called him to show him *"kindness."*

Regardless of our past abuse and hurts, the King of all kings has called to us. His call has been sent out to us as we hide in our places of fear and shame. Of course, our King doesn't need a servant to look for us. He knows where we are in our separation, and He has sent for us.

Even as you read these words, He is speaking healing to your abuse. Neither does our King need a medical report on us. He knows all about our wounds. He was there when the abuse took place. It was not God's intention that someone violate us or cause us pain. It was not the Lord's plan for someone to shatter our trust in other people or to pollute our self-esteem. But He knows every hurt and every point of pain, and it is His desire to restore us.

How does He accomplish that restoration? First He calls us back to Himself. When someone has violated us, we find it difficult to trust anyone, including God Himself. In the case of Mephibosheth, David first had to remove any cause for fear in the heart of Jonathan's son. Our King, Jesus, also speaks to the fear that took hold of our hearts when we were wounded. He speaks to the lie that the enemy planted—the lie that God does not hear us or does not care about us. He reveals the truth: God wants us. So the first step to healing is to realize that the Lord, by His Spirit, is calling us to Himself to heal and restore us.

If we can get that far, if we can believe that the Lord really desires our healing and is calling us, then we must next see what He is calling us to. King David called Mephibosheth to total restoration. In the same way, our King has called us back from Lodebar, the place of name-less separation, to restore all that was ours by birthright. God has purposed that we live in fear and separation no longer. It is no longer necessary that we stuff down the hurts and pretend that they aren't there. He *"has not given us a spirit of fear, but of power and of love and a sound mind"* (2 Timothy 1:7 NKJV).

There is nothing left for us to do but come to the King's table. The King has provided that we eat at His table, that we live in His grace fully healed and restored. We never read of the lameness of Mephibosheth again in the Bible. When Mephibosheth took his place at the table, his crippled legs were no longer of any consequence. His lameness was under the table; they were under the grace and provision of God. There Mephibosheth looked the same as everyone else. We don't know what kinds of defects and wounds may have found their way under that table in David's palace, but at the table of the Lord all are restored. We may still have scars from our past wounds, just as the legs of Mephibosheth were still lame physically. (See 2 Samuel 9:13.) But the King desires to bring total healing to our hearts, so that we might know the grace of God.

A Personal Invitation

Friend, it is no mere chance that you picked up this book. It is your call to healing, to reach out and touch the hem of His garment and be healed forever. So take the first step and believe that you have picked up this book by divine direction. You are called to the King's table by personal invitation. Though you may have been skillful in hiding what was hurting, the King knows the issues with which you struggle. Perhaps you've struggled with some of the same issues that I have, which I described here; perhaps you wrestle with others. Regardless, the Lord has called you to a place of healing and restoration. He has invited you to put those issues under His table and take your place as a son or daughter. (See 2 Samuel

9:11.) Just as He called me, *even with my issues,* the Lord has called you to Himself, to a new season of healing and wholeness in your life. Take hold of the hem of His garment and be healed in Jesus' name.

> *Behold, at that time I will undo all that afflict thee: and I will save her that halteth, and gather her that was driven out; and I will get them praise and fame in every land where they have been put to shame.*
> (Zephaniah 3:19)

Personal Reflections

Epilogue

"Go in Peace"

Epilogue

"Go in Peace"

And He said to her, "Daughter [or son], your faith has made you well. Go in peace, and be healed of your affliction."
—*Mark 5:34 NKJV*

"**G**o in peace...." Peace is the bottom line. Peace—or the lack of it—is the real concern, regardless of the particular issues that plague us. No matter what issues we struggle with, there is a peace for us in Jesus Christ. Perhaps you struggle with some of the same issues I did. Certainly there are many more issues that plague and rob us than just the ones we have discussed in this book. Whatever your issue is, there is only one path to healing, and that path will lead straight to Jesus Christ. *"There is no other name under heaven given among men by which we must be saved*

[healed, restored, made whole]" (Acts 4:12 NKJV). Don't run from Jesus the Christ; run to Him!

When I recall the issues and healing I have experienced in my life and ministry, I believe that there is no issue beyond the concern and compassion of our loving Lord. After all, God has transformed *me* through His love! I have gone from prevaricator to preacher, from fear to faith, from lack to prosperity, from sickness to health, from pride to humility, and more. All of this came out of the love and grace of God through Jesus Christ.

The Lord has the same love for you. Is your issue pride? Allow God to remind you of His great deliverance. Is your issue one of truthfulness? Reach out to the hem of the One who is the truth. Is there emptiness in your life? Then have an encounter with the living Christ and allow Him to fill you. Is your issue one of poverty? Jesus has saved the best wine for this season of your life. Is there a wound from the past causing you to limp into the present? The Lord has a special place of healing and restoration for you at His own table. In all these things, *"let the peace of God rule in your hearts"* (Colossians 3:15).

We all have issues. I ask you again, as I did at the beginning of this book: Are you ready to leave the guilt, the shame, and the separation behind and be healed? God wants to do a new thing in your life. He wants you to reach out to Him. Will you? Jesus is waiting. Whatever the source of your issue, the presence of Jesus Christ is the true and lasting source of healing. He desires to touch you and heal you *even with your issues.*

These things I have spoken to you, that in Me you may have peace. In the world you will have tribulation; but be of good cheer, I have overcome the world. (John 16:33 NKJV)

"Go in peace..."

Personal Reflections

About the Author

———————⚬∞⚬———————

About the Author

*D*r. Wanda A. Turner is an articulate, personable vessel of honor in the kingdom of God. Her unique style, powerful message, and submission to God's call on her life have enabled her to become one of the most sought-after female ministers in the body of Christ. Dr. Turner uses her tenacity and her extraordinary personality to expose and bring healing to the more difficult and painful issues plaguing the people of God.

As she upholds the standards of a virtuous woman, not only has she become the role model for pastors' wives, but she has also become God's blueprint for righteous women the world over.

Dr. Turner's undergraduate studies in music and English at Chapman College and the University of California at Davis have contributed to her excellence in numerous areas of ministry. She majored in Urban Studies at Pepperdine University, obtained a master's degree in psychology from the California Institute, and

151

earned a Doctorate of Divinity at Southern California's School of Ministry in 1985.

Dr. Turner utilizes her excellence in Christian administration, preaching, and teaching the Gospel of Jesus Christ to execute her responsibilities as Associate Pastor and First Lady of Covenant Worship Center of Inglewood, California. She serves as Chief Executive Officer of M.E.C.C.A. Ministries International, which is an evangelical Christian organization of over 200 churches in the United States, Haiti, Trinidad, and the Philippines founded by Bishop Andrew C. Turner II.

This internationally known speaker has ministered at conferences across the country. Dr. Turner's television appearances include the Black Entertainment Television Network. Her life-changing messages have been captured in both book and video formats, including the uncompromising book entitled *Sex Traps*.

Dr. Wanda Turner is the wife of Bishop Andrew C. Turner II, the proud mother of four daughters and the grandmother of five.

Using the Word of God as her road map, this author, wife, mother, and minister continues to establish the framework that will create a contagious desire for women all over the world to be all that God has called them to be.

ANOTHER POWERFUL BOOK
from Whitaker House

The Secret Place
Dr. Dale A. Fife

You hunger to live in the presence of God. You yearn to know the Father's heart in an intimate way. You desire revelation and passionate encounters with the Almighty. You long to spend time in the Secret Place, getting to know the Father in a deeper way. If you long to experience a greater intimacy with the Father, *The Secret Place* will draw you in and change your life!

ISBN: 0-88368-715-1 • Trade • 240 pages

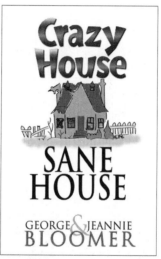

OTHER POWERFUL BOOKS
from Whitaker House

How to Stop the Pain
Dr. James B. Richards

You've been wounded, and you just can't seem to heal. You forgive, but you can't forget! This paradigm-shattering book will free you from the forces that would turn you into a victim. It will lead you step-by-step through a simple process that will free you from the pain of the past and protect you from the pain of the future.

ISBN: 0-88368-722-4 • Trade • 208 pages

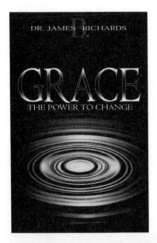

Grace: The Power to Change
Dr. James B. Richards

Christians everywhere have been missing the truth about grace—and living in defeat as a result. Grace is God's ability working in you to do what you cannot. It is the power to change. Take to heart the principles in this book, and discover the dimension of Christian living that Jesus called "easy and light." Relax and let the grace of God change your heart!

ISBN: 0-88368-730-5 • Trade • 192 pages

OTHER POWERFUL OOKS

from Whitaker House

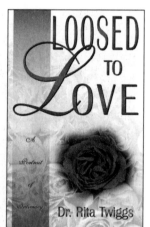

Loosed to Love
Dr. Rita Twiggs

Today you can be set free and walk right into the powerful things God has for you. Join Dr. Rita Twiggs as she shares how you can break free from the bondages that separate you from the Lover of your soul. You can be released to a new level of intimacy with the Father—a relationship in which you completely trust Him and know you satisfy Him. Your God-given destiny awaits you. Discover the powerful purpose for your life.

ISBN: 0-88368-651-1 • Trade • 224 pages

Imprisoned by Secrets of the Heart
Patricia Harris

That dark secret—the one you buried in the deepest recess of your heart, the one you vowed never to reveal to another living soul, the one that makes you cringe every time it pops into your mind.

Whether it's from hurt, shame, abuse, or fear, we all struggle with inner imprisonment. Patricia Harris tackles this subject head-on, providing both moving personal accounts and answers to how you can experience a joy-filled new life as you break free from the secrets of your heart.

ISBN: 0-88368-624-4 • Trade • 192 pages

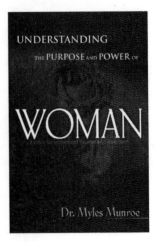
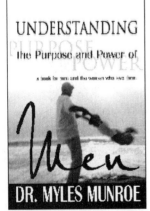

ANOTHER POWERFUL BOOK
from Whitaker House

The Anatomy of God
Dr. Kenneth Ulmer

Throughout Scripture, God describes Himself in anatomical terms we are familiar with. His eyes wink and squint. His mouth whispers, His smile radiates, and He inclines an ear to our cries. In *The Anatomy of God,* Dr. Kenneth Ulmer introduces us to a God who is touchable, emotional, and accessible. If you desire to know God in a deeper way, or even if you question His closeness and concern, allow *The Anatomy of God* to draw you closer to Him.

ISBN: 0-88368-711-9 • Trade • 208 pages

D1259955